More advance praise for
One With the People

"*One With the People* is a rich, rewarding book filled with wisdom that takes the reader to a beautiful level of understanding of leadership through service, and a deeper appreciation of love as our guiding force. With an uplift of pure heart energy, I am moved to the core of my being by the beauty, truth, and love contained within *One With the People*. It is a gift to my heart, and I recommend the experience!"

— **Lisa Morison**

"Dr King has masterfully woven a 'page turning' story into a unique paradigm for leadership."

— **Kevin O'Connor**, Entrepreneur

"Jack King sheds light on the path to successful leadership in his new book *One With the People*. This beautifully written tale comes from the servant heart of one who has great insight and wisdom. Through storytelling and Native American culture, Jack weaves the deeper threads of meaning behind effective leadership. This is a beautiful blueprint for successful living that needs to be shared generously. *One With the People* is written for everyone, and should be shared between parent and child, teacher and student. Jack generously gives us keys to purpose-driven leadership, unleashing the potential that lies within each one of us."

— **Catherine Darnell**, Advocate and Mentor, Hope's Tapestry

"Jack King has created a powerfully passionate story of leadership like none you have ever read before. It is an inspiring story filled with uncommon wisdom and five-star insights. This book will change the way you view leaders and, perhaps, the way you view yourself from this day forward. Within these pages, Jack says what most of us are afraid to admit, yet each of us, in our heart of hearts, yearns to hear: Leadership has everything to do with Love!"
— **Marjorie Sunflower Sargent**, Director of the Foundation for American Heritage Voices and Administrative Director for the Mattaponi Healing Eagle Clinic

"Mix one part storytelling, two parts Native American culture, three parts character-based leadership, and what do you have? *One With the People*, an enchanting and informative leadership book by Jack King. Sani's lessons to Topangah about love, respect, courage, honesty, humility, truth, and wisdom are lessons for us all. Wise lessons about leading ourselves and others. Compelling lessons about the power of heart, love and compassion in making a positive, sustainable difference in how we lead. A joy to read!"
— **Jane Perdue**, co-author of *The Character-Based Leader*

"What Dr King teaches us – to lead you must first love – is a lesson many appointed to leadership just don't get. They will be leaders in name only, for no one will want to be their follower. Only when followers recognise your love and anoint you leader, do you become one. Jack's story illustrates this beautifully, sensitively yet powerfully, & I commend it to anyone wishing to unlock their leadership potential."
— **Tim Douglas**, Commercial HR, UK

"Dr Jack King's book reveals ancient wisdom to a modern world in turmoil and so needing help from the 'elders.' Its powerful teachings have the potential to transform communities, change the way 'leaders' lead, and reach far out across borders around the world to challenge traditional conceptions of the citizen, the state, and international relations. It is an incredibly valuable resource to support the current and burgeoning paradigm shift in human evolution."

— **Sharon Eden**, author of *The Passion Whisperer*

"Jack King's beautifully written book, *One With the People*, instantly struck me as a not-so-ordinary story of extraordinary appeal and value. It's a magical, mystical, very believable tale about two well-developed characters — Sani, a wise Navajo elder, and Topangah, a young, hungry-for-wisdom maiden — and their great respect for the Beauty in all things. This is a book worth multiple reads ... packed with thought-provoking truths about the journey we call life."

— **Nannette Kennedy**, Worldwide Communications Coordinator, Humanity's Team

"Today's organizations need effective leadership, and effective leaders need to practice with Love – Jack King tells a story of love, and how we can grow and prosper using the lessons of Native Americans who have come before."

—— **Dr Stuart E. Gothold**, Clinical Professor Emeritus, USC

NOTE

ONE WITH THE PEOPLE

ONE
WITH THE
PEOPLE

Everything You Need To Be the Leader They Need!

JACK KING

Virginia

Visit www.onewiththepeople.com

Cover/Jacket design by Jack King
Design and composition by Jack King
Author photograph © by Wendy King

Cataloging-in-Publication Data
King, Jack
        One With the People: everything you need to be the leader they need/Jack King.
        — 1ˢᵗ ed.
            215 p.; 22cm.
        ISBN 5-800090-201050
        1. Leadership. 2. Success in business. 3. Leadership Development. 4. Leadership
— Moral and ethical aspects. 5. Indians of North America — Philosophy. 6. Organizational
change — management. 7. New Age Movement. I. Title.

HD57.7   .K56 2012
658.4

ISBN 13: 978-1482658620
ISBN 10: 1482658623

10 9 8 7 6 5 4 3 2 1

Printed in the United States of America

First edition

To my girls,
Gretl, Grace, Hope, & Faith,
and girls everywhere
who shall reclaim lost harmony
and lead us
through the dark night
so we may be awakened,
like the dawn's breaking of a new day,
to the profound possibilities of life, love,
— and leadership —
which invite us to
embrace compassion,
restore goodness,
and become more loving;
profound possibilities
that blend the sacred colors of man
into a single hue of humanity
that shines like a thousand suns.
Peace.

Contents

Author's Note

I am hopeful, for in our midst are those who shall truly lead us. They look like the girl next door and the guy down the street. If we take the time to notice, they look a lot like you and me. Some are old, but far more are not. Some are men, but most are women. Some are well-educated, but all are wise. They are also courageous, honest, and respectful. They are generous, and humble. They understand the connection between heart and head, and they, just like you, are not afraid to love those they serve.

That's why I wrote *One With the People*. You see, deep inside each of us is everything we need to be the leader the people need. Yes, that includes you. Especially you!

When I first put pen to paper, so to speak, some many months ago, I knew I wanted to connect the Ojibwe (Anishinaabe) teachings of the 'seven grandfathers' to leadership. Used together, these grandfathers (love, respect, courage, honesty, humility, truth, and wisdom) illuminate the essence and purpose of our lives. As essential elements of the human spirit, they call out the leader within each of us, giving us the freedom to love so we may give the best of ourselves to others. They help us draw from the joy in doing what we are supposed to do, teaching us what is important so we may come to know how we are to live, how we are to serve, and how we are to lead. They also teach us to overcome our tendency to give too little so we may, in turn, help another find meaning in their life and, thereby, restore harmony to a hurting world as we walk our own path along the Beauty Way. These seven grandfathers, as you will see, are not an end unto themselves; they are, instead, a means to a better world.

The stories rising from these pages are mine, yet they belong to everyone. They are inspired by many teachers — the eight-legged, the six-, the four-, and the two-legged ones, the winged-ones, green-growing beings, those that swim in waters deep, the crawling ones, those that slither among the grasses, the star nations, every pebble and stone, the river and stream, and the rooted one that grows like a tall standing brother — who walk with us, talk with us, and ensure we are never alone.

Across many cultures, storytelling draws its power from the strength of a circle, a place where we are all equal, where no one is in front, no one is behind, no one is above, and no one is below. Storytelling, like the circle, unites us. It forges a common bond. Stories tell us who we were, what we knew, where we came from, and where we are going. They reflect our life as it was, and as it is. They give us insights into what life might become. Stories talk to community. They explain how life came to be, and why and how we celebrate it. Stories teach. Stories inspire. Stories encourage. Stories motivate. Some stories take but a moment to share; others need generations to express the wonder and majesty of our journey, a journey without beginning or end, a small part of the greater whole. Our work — to find our voice — is a life's journey that lies somewhere in between. As you read the stories, let me encourage you to seek the silence of the moment so you can best determine where your love, as a leader, is most needed. As you do, be not afraid to summon the strength of character to be one with the people like the soaring eagle is one with the wind.

In closing, I have written this book with the utmost respect for all indigenous traditions. I mean only to bring honor to each of these traditions and, perhaps, to offer a path for healing among the misgivings of humanity.

mi'taku'ye o'yasin,

Jack King (Charlottesville, Virginia)

Prologue

"Flowers do not force their way with great strife.
Flowers open to perfection slowly in the sun."
~White Eagle, Ponca (Sioux)

They asked us to be there early on Wednesday morning. They said it was important. Really important. There was no time to go into it now. "Just come," they said.

Aside from getting an earlier than normal start, my Wednesday began much like any other day at the office. Admittedly, it feels somewhat rushed. Perhaps a bit on the dull side. Some might even call it drab. Of note, the predictability of the day drips with a stale uncertainty. That is, until the oven-hot, made-from-scratch, catered New York bagels and fresh roasted gourmet coffee arrives.

The rich, luxurious conference room is anything but drab. I'd describe it as eccentric. Rare, tropical Brazilian hardwoods, for the most part hand-carved, immediately catch the eye. Large, diamond-tucked, black leather armchairs and an over-sized oval table overstate a presumptuous opulence. Commissioned, museum quality, hand-painted oil portraits of past company presidents, each mounted and displayed in a meticulously crafted solid alder frame with a distressed gold-gilt finish, hang conspicuously on the walls. Faux plants pretend to attach a free-spirited ambiance in a formal, classical room where, at its essence, yin meets yang. The warm, complex plum carpet nicely offsets the gilded golden frames surrounded by untoned mauve hues of mid-nineteenth century African mallow flower fame. Three laptops sit, each neatly stacked one on top of another, near the head of the table. A console under the table's edge controls two high definition 3D 3LCD multimedia projectors hung from the ceiling panel over the center of the room, a retractable 108-inch flexible projection screen, a custom-built sliding whiteboard and screen cover, assorted lights, a multimedia suite, and ancillary audio. The view, for those fortunate to sit on the east side of the room, is magnificent. The famed Blue Ridge Mountains, accented by regal rays of the morning sun, fill the picture glass windows as only a province of the larger Appalachian range can, with sweeping shades of gold, green, orange, red and, of course, blue. A very distinctive slate blue, created naturally by the isoprene emitted into the atmosphere by the many large hickory, poplar, and stunted oak trees throughout the range, captivates the soul. Autumn has arrived in full regalia; now is the time for change. The colors painted along each ridge face are vibrant, breathtaking. If only the same could be said about the people — and the organization they love — assembled inside that conference room.

But this was to be no ordinary Wednesday. What happened had a profound impact on me; in just a few short hours, ephemeral moments that deepened my convictions and reignited my passions, my heart, and my life were forever changed. Our community and, by extension, how we perceive others, was also changed by the shared experience. I am certain those hours that changed us can change you, too.

Carter Anhalt, the organization's long-time principal partner, called the meeting to order. All eyes were upon her as she began, and ended, the meeting with a single sentence:

"The love is gone."

The room drew terribly silent and uncomfortably warm. Some minutes passed as Carter gauged the impact of her message on the faces of those present. During those precious moments, I recalled something my wise and aged neighbor, Fairlight White Wolf, told me some weeks earlier: "Silence tells us a great many things. The end of silence tells us even more."

Armed with Fairlight's insight, I sat waiting for the silence to end.

To my surprise, I discovered sitting in an awkward silence is, at once, both difficult and easy. Just a month earlier, I would have been prompted by my impatience to break the silence myself thinking something, anything, needed to be said. Truth is, sometimes it is better to say nothing.

Carter stood and left the room. Many followed her out. The few remaining finished their hasty conversations before going on about their business.

I remained seated, waiting for everyone to leave. Then, I listened. Intently. It was in the silence of that eccentric room with a panoramic view on a very ordinary Wednesday morning that the extraordinary occurred; I began to hear what was always there.

Fairlight was right.

Work would have to wait. An hour later, Fairlight joined me at a local coffee shop. Although it was early, we opted to enjoy lunch. The specials are fabulous. My favorite is roasted turkey rubbed with olive oil, garlic, and rosemary, on country wheat with brie, mayonnaise, cranberry sauce, and lettuce. Fairlight orders smoked turkey on sourdough with goat cheese spread, cucumbers, red onions, and alfalfa sprouts. Both of us opt for a golden brown, sweetly wholesome, freshly baked cookie made from whole oats, coconut, honey, and brown sugar for a tasty snack after the meal.

While we wait for our meal to be served, I share the morning's news and observations with Fairlight, asking her to offer any first impressions and insights. She reacts without hesitation, purposefully side-stepping first impressions altogether to tell me exactly what I need to hear.

"Life is a most wonderful story," she begins. After a short pause, she continues, "Stories are all we have. Yet we do not possess them. They are given to us that we might share them. Stories teach, and they help us learn. Some stories motivate, guide, influence, and inspire us. Without ceremony, they find a place somewhere between who we are and who we think we are, and there they speak to our heart. Stories stand, unwavering, at the crossroads of our life, their power ready to enchant and delight, touch and teach, call and challenge. Stories bridge where we are to where we need to be; they give people the courage to face their fear, and to go on. Everyone, after all, has overcome some fear, and each of us has a story to tell. Sometimes our story requires no words; at other times, as our people have said many times, it takes a thousand voices to tell that story."

"Fairlight, I am so glad you are here. Do you remember talking with me about silence, and telling me how much we can hear when silence draws to a close?"

"Of course," Fairlight remarks. "Do you know why I said those things?"

"*Why?*"

"Yes. Do you know why the end of silence tells us so much?"

"No. I don't suppose I do."

"Let me see if I can help." After a long pause, Fairlight begins, "Life is all about the present moment. Stories help us understand how we got to that moment. They honor life. They also honor earth, wind, fire, and water. You see, stories are rooted in Mother Earth. And so, too, is silence. Between man and his heart lies a great gulf. Silence fills the void. And love fills the silence. Stories well-told bud and bloom, nourished by the love bridging that expanse and bringing the melody of silence to our ears."

"That sounds beautiful, Fairlight, but what does it mean?"

With an uncommon restfulness, Fairlight reflects on the meaning behind her friend's question before her words fall softly onto a waiting heart. "As we look first to the North, then the East, South, and West, before turning our eyes Above and Below, we turn our attention to our center and we begin to see we are never alone. Life surrounds us; creatures that swim in waters deep, the flying ones, the crawling ones and those that slither among the grasses, and every two-, four-, six-, eight-, and many-legged brother and sister know their course. We can see how each star, ocean, pebble and stone, field and orchard, spring, river and stream, woodland, and the rooted one that rises like a tall standing brother has its own place upon Mother Earth."

The words had not quite sunk in when Fairlight closes her eyes, and solemnly whispers, "Only man has lost his way. And only balance and harmony can restore his bearings."

"Where can we find this balance and harmony, Fairlight?"

"One doesn't find balance or harmony; balance and harmony find us, often through our stories of life and love. A never-ending circle of life, and an ever-present love found in every flower and tree, every plant and animal, every person from the four sacred colors, every fish and bird. If we but stop, look, and listen, we can rediscover the way everywhere."

"We *see* them, Fairlight?"

"Yes. Of course, we can often hear them, too. But the best stories can be seen. Some are carved into trees or on canyon walls. Others are scratched or painted onto ivory, stones, clay, bones, hides, leaves, paper, or wood. Some stories are recorded on film while others are etched into our hearts. All of them help us in some small way to foster community, engage our imagination, enrich our lives, restore hope, invoke wonder, and/or bring together the young and the old that we may affirm spiritual truths, share knowledge, connect generations, and weave together the timeless wisdom of diverse cultural beliefs across, throughout, and beyond time where some part of us can live happily ever after. To tell a story is to reclaim lost harmony, to teach the goodness of *all* life."

"That is so beautiful, Fairlight."

"There is a story of kindness and generosity in each of us, a story of love. Such stories structure our existence, bearing a strong impact on where we are and who we are. We see this in our dances, our prayers, and our drawings, in our poetry, our music, our songs, and our declarations. Story is an enduring voice, a collective voice, fashioned in the vessel we call life. It carries us, and makes us who we are because it belongs to a shared humanity. At its essence, story redresses the balance; it sets things right. We and the stories become one. Our stories wrap around the old way, to shape us and to fill us with respect, forgiveness, sharing, and the power of love. Stories are in our bones and in our hearts; we are in their breath. They nourish us and, like them, we, too, grow with each telling, with each new act of love."

"In the busy-ness of life, Fairlight, I think many of us forget just how prevalent, and necessary, stories are to communities near and far."

"Why do you think stories are necessary?"

"That's simple, Fairlight. Storytelling transforms lives."

"Can you tell me more?"

"Yes, of course. As we both know, stories abound; their impact is often unconstrained. We rely on them every day in every facet of life: art, law, medicine, education, business, and community calls to action, to name a few. Storytelling is as old as humanity itself. It clearly predates recorded history, and we see evidence of its use around the world. Every culture exists, in part, because of the stories others needed to tell. Storytelling opens our minds to new horizons, to the realm of possibility comfortably nestled deep within the dominion of the impossible. Storytelling is powerful. It invites the listener to develop an intimate awareness; it nourishes the imagination. It honors life; like an enlightened awareness, it grooms connection and builds relationships. The stories we tell often exist across many dimensions; their meaning extends from the toils of everyday life to the extravagance of the divine. They embrace power befitting kings, power that transcends time, matter, and space. Storytelling brings out the best in us; somehow, something emerges from within, Fairlight, to help us discover context in our past, explore new paths, and find our place."

"I couldn't agree more. Finding our place gives us a point of origin to share common ground with others, to build communities, and to make new friends. Yet, finding the voice behind our story is not enough; we must use it to tell our story. After all, we live in stories; our place within them helps us to see our past in transforming ways, to learn from each other, and to celebrate our diverse experiences. Each of us brings a story other hearts want to hear. We look for its deeper meaning and we invite it to take hold of us. In the comfort of its embrace, we can let go knowing it remains with us. Like our singing and dancing, our stories touch us profoundly; they teach love. Stories belong to the one telling them, yet they connect all of us, lifting vibrant colors from the palette of one life to paint the poignant pages of another's life."

"Do our stories always have to involve others, Fairlight?"

"Though there are some who would rather believe we're in this all alone, I prefer the alternative view that teaches it's not about me. We (all things) coexist in the circle of life. One, no more important than another, depends upon the other so each of us may come to realize and experience our many relationships, to love beyond our fear, and to walk in balance."

"So we may find the love again?"

"Precisely. It is up to us, especially if the people have chosen to follow us, to let our love expect and demand nothing, but fulfill everything, at least for a moment, for another. As you and I know, it is not leaders the people seek; they seek to know love. When we find the courage to step away from our fear, we can more easily see it is for the sake of love one leads. In truth, there's no other reason. Those who have made the journey from their heads to their hearts, and back again, understand how to lead with love. Only they who speak from their heart can truly lead the people to the love they, too, seek; the people will follow no other."

"Please tell me more, Fairlight."

"Sure. I'm happy to do that. I recall a particular story I heard many times growing up. It's a story of profound leadership. What I appreciate most about the story is its sacred link between the material and spiritual realm of leadership that, in the end, brings the two together as a seamless whole. Circular, not linear; sacred, not secular. The setting is a four-day vision quest, of sorts, on the top of a grand mesa in the four corners region of America's southwest. In this story, Sani, a very old and very wise Navajo man, prepares his adopted granddaughter, Topangah, a young Tongva lady of twelve winters, to take her place among the people and lead them to a new and better place. Sani uses the Anishinaabe teachings of *Seven Grandfathers* to help Topangah understand what is truly necessary to lead: love, respect, courage, honesty, humility, truth, and wisdom. A different animal embodies the teachings of each virtue. If it's okay with you, I'd like to pick up the story late on the first morning after Sani and Topangah have found their way to their temporary home on top of the mesa where they soon discover they are not alone ..."

1
Love: Be as the Soaring Eagle ~ One With the Wind

A very great vision is needed for life,
and the man who has it
must follow it — as the eagle seeks the deepest blue of the sky.
~Crazy Horse, Oglala Lakotah

The young girl of 12 winters stopped, careful not to make another sound. She heard it again, and she wanted to know its significance. But who would she ask? Suddenly, a very old Navajo man of great beauty stood before her, appearing as though he came down from Father Sky. She knew there was nothing to fear; their friendship is a sacred one. So, she asked him.

"Sani," she whispered.

'Yes, Topangah," Sani replied. "What is it?"

"You are *hataalii*, a healer, Sani. You are the center that receives power and gives it to any who are in need. You see how body, mind, and spirit are connected, not simply within a single being, but across families, communities, relations, Earth Mother, and the universe. You know what it is like to care for another more than you care for yourself."

"Yes, Topangah. That is what I do."

"I know, Sani. But I don't mean it that way."

"What *do* you mean, Topangah?"

"Well, I think there's more to it than that. So much more. I watch you. And I pay attention. You don't put others first because you have to. You do so because it is your nature. You understand the natural order of things, Sani. Mother Earth and Father Sky have taught you the necessity and the importance of maintaining balance and harmony with your surroundings, with the world around you, and with yourself. We see this balance and harmony in your love and compassion, and in your giving and receiving. That's why the people have chosen you to lead us. You have come to know more than many will ever learn. Because you help us understand every chant, every offering, and every action has meaning, your ways bring together balance, symmetry, respect, harmony, and connectedness to lift us. Your ways are humble and honest. Your ways are wise; they reflect the deep respect you have for our people. Your ways invite us to be our best."

"Yes, Topangah. The people call it *hózhó*, or *hózhóni*; you might hear some say I 'walk in beauty.' It is the way of living a balanced and harmonious life where everything — people, spirit, and nature — is connected, and influences everything else. It enables me to lead, not simply because the people have asked me to lead them, but because the people see in me a reflection of our multi-dimensional world, a world of one where every relation is important to the next because it is in touch with all aspects of one's world; the people see in me a way of life."

"Yes, Sani. But it's even more than that, isn't it?"

"What are you saying, Topangah?"

"Sani, I can see the path to becoming a medicine man — a singer, a healer, a spiritual teacher, and a leader — is not easy. Because it is full of trials and tribulations, suffering and sacrifice, challenges, and learning, it requires patience, understanding, and compassion. It surely must encompass all facets of life and human nature, extending beyond the physical to include the mental, emotional, and spiritual aspects of our lives."

"You have learned much, Topangah. As you have reasoned, it is for me to take on the suffering and the fear, the hate and the anger, the pain and the confusion, and the sickness of our people. Like the season of new life, traditional ceremonies, medicine, sacred dances, and ancient rituals come to my aid."

"Sani, I believe there is something more."

"Yes, Topangah."

"Sani, you are *hataalii*, our singer, healer, and spiritual teacher — our leader — because you are not afraid to love us."

Looking up to *Yádilhil Shitaá* (Father Sky), Topangah smiles. High above the broad piñon trees near the crest of the colorful mesa, her friend, Eagle, circles higher and higher over valleys, fields, and mountains like the smoke offered to Great Spirit rises from the pipe to carry our prayers from the physical world to the spirit world. She has seen him many times before. Each time, he appears to know she is near and calls for her as only he can: E-e-e-ya! E-e-e-ya! And each time she hears his cry, she looks to Above World with an angelic smile.

Eagle is her friend. He represents everything good about her life. In Eagle, Topangah sees and learns of love. She asks Sani, a wise old tribal leader gifted as a 'word sender' and the ancient art of storytelling, what it all means.

"Sani, why does Eagle soar with such grace and purpose?"

"Little Topangah," replied Sani, "Eagle makes no effort to be. He simply is."

"Can we fly with him?," Topangah asks. After a short pause to reflect, Sani affirms, "You already do. Walk with me."

It is not a long walk, but it is a beautiful one! Stepping over stones along the Wolven trails, Sani and his adopted granddaughter, Topangah, soon reach the mesa's glorious expanse. They stop to fully absorb the majesty. Sitting with their legs not merely touching, but clearly in touch with *Shimá Nahasdzáán* (Mother Earth), they look again to Father Sky's deep blue palette.

"Topangah," Sani softly speaks with a rather sacred solemnity, "although it is not for you to know the passing of times I have seen, keep your eyes on our friend, Eagle, as I talk of the important duty that befalls man."

Topangah, serenely and comfortably sitting with her legs tightly crossed under her small frame, learned early on from her Elders the importance of being close to Mother Earth. Her grandmother fondly remembered the days of her youth, and often spoke of lessons learned over a lifetime. "Our people, the *Diné*," recounted her grandmother, "love the ground upon which they sit. It is a reminder of one's closeness to maternal power. Within the warmth of earth, one finds strength, healing, cleanliness, and a restful peace."

Topangah could not mistake the strong smells of wildness, the desert, and her people as she quietly considered her grandmother's soft voice and the warmth of her words of encouragement in the voice of the wind. Lost in the moment, she unexpectedly found herself face to face with the sound she heard before, the sound that first drew her to Sani. With her concentration broken, Topangah wanted more than ever to understand what it was she heard. Sani was not stirred from his contemplation but, she noticed, perhaps for the first time, her friend Eagle heard it, too, as he continued to paint endless circles onto Father Sky's deep blue, cloudless canvas.

"Topangah." Sani's voice was as the thunder that breaks the silent vigil at storm's edge. "Our Elders teach us many things about life. From our earliest years, we learn life, not unlike the path our friend, Eagle, now takes as he sails upward out of man's grasp, is a circle extending from childhood to childhood. From our Lakotah, Nakotah, and Dakotah brothers in the north, we learn all things in the circle are equal. The circle creates unity, not just among men of every sacred color — white, yellow, red, and black — but we find a place on the circle for all living things: every animal, every tree, every plant, and every man, woman, and child. And just like every other living being, we generally leave this world much as we entered it. The difference is what we learn along the way. For many, their learning accounts for so little. For others, their learning makes all the difference, not only for them but, more importantly, for the rest of us. Do you know why, Topangah?"

Topangah could not express the answer Sani sought. But she knew his words to be true. She saw it in her people. And she saw how her people might be drawn to one more than any other. Sani was the perfect example. They did not draw to him because they sought healing. They were drawn to him because he understood the people and their needs, and he believed in them. He knew their strengths and weaknesses, and he knew about power, love, reality, healing, and life. He believed in the power of a positive attitude. He looked to their future as he looked for the good in everyone. He encouraged them, he valued them, and he cared about them.

They were drawn to him because he loved them.

Topangah whispers, "Love?"

Topangah and Sani look heavenward to Above World. As they do, Eagle looks upon them. Time stands still as Grandfather Sun dances with Mother Earth across Father Sky.

Sani again breaks the silence. "Like Grandfather Sun, Topangah, we come. We stand in the footprints of our Elders as we walk. Sometimes we dance. We heal someone's hurt. We restore another's hope. We leave. Yet, we remain, always close by!"

Topangah thought for a moment. "How can we leave yet always be close by, Sani? Is it because our people know us, and remember?"

"Yes," says Sani. "And, no. They know us, but knowing is not enough. They remember, but memory fades, just as Grandfather Sun's setting rays disappear each night beyond the canyon rim."

Topangah was wrestling with this idea when Sani spoke again. "Topangah, the air you breathe does not belong to you. It belongs to all living things, those now in your presence, those yet to come, and those who came before you. The words you speak travel the winds that have brushed the hair of young girls in faraway places, in times distant and near. The bones of our Elders, in their journey to the other side, have provided nutrient to trees that shade all who now walk under their branches, and all who shall walk there in the days and nights to come."

Topangah urges Sani to stop. The full explanation will have to wait because the view over the mesa has carried her to a new place, a place of deeper understanding. "Sani," Topangah says with a smile. "Gifts given with no regard for anything in return bring remembrance of the giver. As we can see, Grandfather Sun brightens the day for all the same. It has been this way since the beginning. And behold our friend, Eagle: those who will take notice soon discover he warmly smiles down upon all. He is wise; he sees everything in the heavens and all things on Mother Earth. For this, he is held in high esteem and the people regard him with much respect."

Sani, delighted with Topangah's discovery, waits a moment before adding, "It is not because he gifts us with his presence that we remember him, Topangah."

As she ponders Sani's remark, it comes to her. "Of course, Sani. We learn from our childhood to respect the gift — and the giver — because *love* connects us."

"Yes, Topangah," Sani kindly whispers as he continues to look skyward. "Love and friendship speak to our kinship with soaring eagles, and it is this love that gives us reason to remember. It is a story shared by all peoples upon Mother Earth."

Both sit enjoying the moment.

A little time passes when Sani asks, "Who do the people seek out to lead them?"

Topangah knew, immediately, who they sought. "They seek those who are unafraid to love them. Like you, Sani."

"Yes, Topangah," Sani acknowledges. "They seek those who are unafraid to love them, and the message that pours out from within their hearts is no different than the yearning of your own. It is the same as the cry of many hearts who have walked before us. Each heart seeks the same thing. To know love. This is no different for our friend, Eagle. His knowing, we learn, comes from his giving. And it is in his giving *we* come to know what he already knew. Love is the driving force that feeds our hopes, our expectations, our songs, and our dreams."

"You see, Topangah," Sani continues, "The people don't seek leaders, they seek to know love. And it is the power of that love shared between them that gives rise to leadership. Like the medicine man who knows his gifts, talents, and knowledge do not rise from his own power but, instead, belong to the people so, too, do true leaders recognize — and appreciate — it is they who are empowered, not the other way around. A true tribal leader assumes a leadership position, not because they sought it but, rather, because that leadership role has chosen him or her. A real medicine man or medicine woman, not unlike any other authentic leader of the people, should never have to identify him/herself as such. It is not the Indian way."

Topangah does not want Sani to stop. She is not certain why Sani has singled her out, but she is certain she is not alone in her eagerness and her desire to learn more. She and her young friends have always looked up to those who lead them with love. (For Topangah, it was always more than merely a mark of respect.) But do they know why? What is it they see when the look up to them? Before now, Topangah would open her eyes but she did not see. Though she now *sees*, is seeing everything? Could there be something more than spiritual knowledge, tribal myths and legends, healing arts, rituals, and ceremonies?

Topangah couldn't say she never gave it much thought. Truth is, from a very young age, she lived in her own little world, a world of color, sound, and movement that danced within dreams that later became tools for self-discovery, spiritual self-development, and healing. Though she knew little to nothing of sacred naming rituals, tobacco burning ceremonies, doctoring ceremonies, sweat lodge ceremonies, potlatches, moontime rituals, spiritual training, vision quests, story-telling sessions, or talking circles, she knowingly possessed a gentleness, understanding, sensitivity, and gift of compassion beyond her years. It is as though the way she *sees* and the way she understands has always been with her. Topangah now, more than ever, wanted to know what *they* see. Do her leaders see *her*? She knows Sani sees her, but what of the others? What do they see in her? What does Sani see in her? Why do the people choose to follow only certain ones?

It is at that moment Sani breaks the silence.

"Topangah, when you look up to a leader of our people, what do you see? What do your young friends see?"

"Sani," she replies, "I now see that they *see*."

Sani smiles.

Continuing, Topangah adds, "Perhaps for the first time, I realize I matter to them. I am not just one of many. And our people matter to them, too. They begin their work from where we are, not where they want us to be. We matter enough for them to honor and respect our experiences, to affirm and connect our identity with our culture, and to say yes to our asking them to lead us."

"Yes, Topangah. It's quite simple really. Leaders do what they do because people matter. The people matter because *love* matters."

Topangah concentrates on Sani's words, but says nothing.

"Let me help you understand, Topangah. Leadership is not a thing. Nor is it a way of life. Leadership knows nothing of position, power, or prominence. It is not self-seeking, nor is it self-serving. Are you listening, Topangah? Do you understand? I'm not suggesting it 'shouldn't be;' I'm saying leadership cannot be these things." Continuing, Sani makes the point more clearly: "At its heart, Topangah, leadership is love manifest, and leadership without love is no leadership at all. Consider our friend, Eagle."

"I love Eagle, Sani," Topangah interjects. "As Eagle soars, my consciousness merges with his so I may be one with him, relaxed, happy, and at peace. His strength inspires me. Eagle is my friend, and he knows my thoughts."

"Topangah, Eagle sees what we cannot see. The Elders tell us he sits in the East with the direction of leadership and courage, emotion, and fire. Eagle, is important to us not because he seeks greatness but, rather, because he avoids its attachment; he shows us why we must love to lead."

"Sani," Topangah asks, "is that all our Elders teach about Eagle?"

"There is much more," Sani tells Topangah. "To know Eagle is to know the Creator, to feel a deep, abiding, brotherly love, the love most visible in humanity. Eagle teaches us a love shared with others must derive its strength from love of oneself, a love that draws on our love for the Great Spirit. We learn Eagle, because he can reach higher into the heavens than all the creatures, was chosen by the Great Spirit to represent this lasting truth. Eagle *is* love."

Sani stops briefly to watch Topangah. Then he adds, "Eagle reflects everything we hold dear. In Eagle, we see power, beauty, skill, a life in harmony with nature, the ability to see into the hearts and minds of the *Diné*, a reason to nurture and care for another, and loyalty. Topangah, the Elders speak of Eagle with a great respect. As Eagle seeks the deepest blue of Father Sky, it is said he lights our *good red road* as it winds its way through the heavens, spilling over the star people onto our sacred mountain tops, and rolling down to find a home among the *Diné* before being lifted to Above World in our songs and prayers to complete its journey, a continuous circle of life, a sacred hoop. In so doing, we may not be able to see Eagle, but he can always see himself. Such is the lesson for our life. The Ancients tell us the good red road is a road of humility and understanding where one stands on equal ground with all others. The river that runs by it is wise and the wind that blows over it knows all things. To know the good red road is to know sacrifice and to always know we can do better. As we walk the good red road, the beauty in all things becomes clear. It is here we pray, dance, think, dream, teach, learn, grieve, and sing. It is here we see the truth in our oneness. Let us always be mindful of what we can see in ourselves even if others cannot see us."

"Please tell me more, Sani," Topangah implores.

"Like the soaring eagle is one with the wind, Topangah," Sani continues, "leaders must be one with the people. Just as the wind lifts Eagle, it is for the leader to lift the people. Even the eagle feather says, 'I will do good things for my people.' In turn, it is the power of the people that becomes the wind beneath the leader's wings. Without this power, the leader can no longer soar. With this power, the people soar, too. High above the tops of the mountains visited by Grandfather Sun. What do you think this power is, Topangah?"

By now, Topangah is hanging on Sani's every word. Her response is immediate. "It is love, Sani."

"Through this love, Topangah, Eagle teaches something more." Topangah's eyes are wide with anticipation as Sani enlightens her. "From Eagle, we learn the language Grandfather Sun shares with those mountains. It is the sound that brings order to the chaos of our world. It is the sound that brings right to our wrongs. It is the sound of silence."

"That's it, Sani! That's what I heard."

"What did you hear, Topangah?"

"Silence, Sani. It was so beautiful!"

"It is beautiful," Sani repeated. "The Elders teach us silence is respected, and courtesy is expected. Silence, they tell us, is not the absence of activity but the evidence of it. It is in this silence we come to understand what it is our heart seeks: the opportunity to serve. And it is in this service a man's 'greatness' is revealed. You see, Topangah, our heart brings to life the story we need to hear as silence waits with us. Silence is a sign of acceptance, serenity, peace, and harmony between man and nature. The Lakotah of the Plains teach us silence produces courage, patience, dignity, and respect for all living things. The man who turns from silence, we learn, turns from his people. Our brothers say it like this: "Man's heart away from nature becomes hard." Teachings of the Chippewa, timber people to the north, urge us to listen in silence to all teachers of the wild — mountains, streams, fields, waterfalls, lightning, thunder, trees, animals, and all living things — so we may learn. In this way, one may inherit the wisdom important for our people, even if our people are not yet ready for us. For, you see, some will make fun of us, others will talk bad about us, while still others may not understand our powers and knowledge come from our relations with nature."

This was a lot for Topangah to grasp. She had much to learn but she was exceedingly grateful for all Sani and Eagle will teach her. She had questions, but she knew the answers were before her. She somehow sensed she had only to listen to her friend to learn from him. And as she watched — and celebrated — her friend soaring unfettered in his blue heavenly realm, she sought, through the power of love, the same freedom to fly, strong and noble, among dreams of her own.

"O' Great Spirit, let me learn to listen," Topangah whispered as Sani stood alone in the stillness to keep a hushed vigil on Grandfather Sun, "so I can help the people

begin to better understand the world that surrounds us —
Grandfather Sun, the stars shining in the indigo sky, Moon
Woman, the wind through the forest, the sacred mountains,
the rivers, lakes, and streams, the animals, both two-legged
and four, and the winged creatures."

"O' Great Spirit, you have taught me the power of Eagle
is also the power of the messenger. Let me learn to listen so I
can help the people begin to find themselves as one with the
life that empowers us — Mother Earth, the wind, the water,
and the fire."

"O' Great Spirit, let me learn to listen so I can help the
people begin to give back like the boundless blue of Father
Sky and the clouds illuminated by Grandfather Sun's rising
give of themselves freely to us."

"O' Great Spirit, let me learn to listen so I can help the
people cause no unnecessary pain to the living. Let me learn
to listen so I can help the people learn to love — and respect
— again."

2
Respect: Stand as the Buffalo ~ Face to Face Against the Ageless Winds of Adversity

The buffalo represents the people and the universe and should always be treated with respect. For was he not here before the two-legged peoples, and is he not generous in that he gives us our homes and our food? The buffalo is wise in many things, and thus we should always be as a relative with him.

~Hehaka Sapa (Black Elk)
Wichasha Wakan (Holy Man) and
Heyókȟa (sacred clown) of the Oglala Lakotah

As the shadows ran across the vast sea of grass like the echo of a gentle whisper, Sani and Topangah lost themselves to the precious, awe-inspiring moments graciously gifted upon the soft earth colors of the mesa with Grandfather Sun's elegant dance across Father Sky. Both sat in silent admiration of all around them. A rich and beautiful plain lay before them. At a little distance, hues of gold, red, brown, and the color-of-the-setting-sun filled their senses. The mesa was soon ablaze with the flash of fireflies flitting under the ever watchful eye of Moon Woman. It is Topangah who finally breaks the hushed stillness of their watchful wonder.

"Why must we come here, Sani? Everything is so beautiful, but we could just as easily have sat under the branches of the large tangle of willows by the river's edge."

"Ah, yes, Topangah. But it is not *us* who must look across this vast mesa. It is *you* that must find your place among our people, among our relations, and among the spirits others cannot see or hear. There is a great learning that awaits you. And it will begin before you and I depart this place. What you discover here — the strength to confront danger and the wisdom to understand fear for what it is — will set you upon a journey no other can make. It is as it should be."

"Where am I going, Sani?"

"That depends on you, Topangah. How you respond to your calling will determine the journey set out before you.

Some become dancers or basket-makers or seers. Others become tracers or doctors. Some are called to sing. You will know before you get there."

"How will I know?"

"Topangah, the journey you must make is not one of dusty trails, gnarled rimrock, sage plains, youthful braided rivers, dark canyons, deep valleys, distant foothills, weathered buttes, cratered highlands, steep-walled mesas, or prairies filled with shale ridges, old oxbows, and wooded draws adorned with snowberry, chokecherry, hawthorn, buffaloberry, and wild plums. The journey you must make knows nothing of the western crested wheatgrass, white poppies, big bluestem, wild sunflowers, milkweed, crisp buffalo grass, silvery sage, purple coneflower, blue gramma, and great stinging nettle swaying to the rhythm of whistling winds. The journey you must make cannot take flight like the meadowlark, sharp-tailed grouse, harrier, longspur, white-crowned sparrow, curlew, bunting, dove, thrasher, tanager, bluebird, towhee, shrike, finch, dickcissel, heron, kestrel, or wren. Yours is a journey that takes you deep within. It calls for the daring of the jay, the carefulness of the crow, and the indomitable spirit of the chickadee."

"In where, Sani?"

"Topangah, living in a way that shows respect for all of creation is vitally important. We have learned from Elders among the Plains people the longest road one must walk is a road they must walk alone." Gently pointing with his long, gnarled, but peacefully aged finger, Sani continues, "It is a walk from here to here. From your head to your heart."

"How long does this journey take, Sani?"

"To journey from the head to the heart takes a lifetime for some, Topangah, but requires a first step from all. To speak to our people as their leader requires something more; you must make the return journey."

"A return journey? From where?"

"Yes, Topangah. From the heart back to the head." Again, pointing his well-aged finger, Sani tells Topangah, "Look there. What do you see?"

Straining, Topangah finds herself at an uncertain crossroad. "Sani, what is it you want me to see? There is nothing before me that is not at once all around me on this mesa."

"You are right, Topangah. And you are mistaken."

"Help me to see, Sani."

"To lead, you must know where you are and where you come from. To do that, you have only to look through the eyes of the people. Past, present, and future. Before you now is the potential for what lies ahead tomorrow. All because of what was there before. *See* Tatanka, Topangah."

"Tatanka?"

"Yes, Topangah. Tatanka. Tatanka represents the moving of the things of the past into our future. Let me help you understand. Our Plains brothers and sisters use *Tatanka* to mean 'buffalo.' A bull buffalo, to be more precise. Our people say, *ayani*. But Tatanka means much more than *ayani*. The peoples of the Plains celebrate Tatanka with a sacred reverence. In the days of your grandmother's grandmother, as many as 30-60 million buffalo roamed the Plains. For reasons we can never fully understand, that number continues to get smaller and smaller."

"That is such sad news, Sani."

"Topangah, Tatanka lies at the center of two cultures. The one depends on him, while the other sees him as the means to an unthinkable end. For both, Tatanka represents a shared destiny."

After giving Topangah a few moments to reflect upon the deeper meanings of Tatanka, Sani gently nudges her with these words: "Tatanka is bigger than all of us, Topangah. He is a symbol of our chance to move forward with guidance, strength, visions, power, and songs."

"But how, Sani?"

"Think upon Buffalo, Topangah. Imagine the magnificence of his presence and the importance of the herd to his survival. We do not see them go their individual ways here and yonder as there is no reason for them to push or force; instead, they willingly take the path that establishes the deepest connection with Mother Earth for all of them. They walk a sacred path, Topangah, as one, honoring all living things. For Tatanka, it has never mattered whether there are 30-60 million, 1,000, or four hundred thousand. Their collective needs are met knowing abundance is present only when, with gratitude, they honor all relations as sacred. Tatanka possesses strength of character that gives rise to his humble, graceful, and peaceful presence. Tatanka's greatness, Topangah, rests in his gentle, generous spirit. He sacrificed his powers for the sake of the people, giving of himself without restraint that others may freely benefit from his gifts of sustenance the people needed to survive."

As a black, quilted night begins to tenderly fall down over the mesa, Eagle, can be heard in the distance, reminding Topangah we can achieve nothing alone and that we should be ever mindful, and grateful, for those gifts that find their way to us.

It has been a long day, a day filled with discovery. Sani suggests rest. For Sani, rest will come with little sleep. As he looks up into the heavens, he thinks of those who need his help, his healing touch. He also thinks of those to come who he cannot help. He gains comfort in the knowledge Topangah will be there for them. In the serenity of the night sky, he finds respite in the millions of stars that shine in Above World. Like the stars, Sani understands he, too, is made of light, the same light that creates the stars, the pure light of love. Most of the night, his eyes will remain open, not out of fear but, rather, because of his resolute trust in all living things.

Sani, mindful of Topangah's servant heart, softly whispers a blessing upon her and her sleep.

Topangah, of course, can do little more than think of Sani, her new friend, Eagle, and all she has seen and heard this first day on top of the mesa standing tall among sandstone spires and great red buttes speckled with green juniper trees. Tatanka weighs heavy on her heart. With profound contemplation under the vigilant eye of Moon Woman, Topangah watches the star nations gently 'shower' her from their place in Above World. She soon falls into a deep, restful sleep. Sometime after night-middle-made and before sunrise, a gentle dream drifts by to keep her company. It is a dream unlike any she has known. Within its soften-edged presence, a very beautiful, unassuming bird messenger sings to her from its perch on a nearby branch. Often, the guardian spirit gives us a special, sacred song. Not knowing if that is the case now, there is a delicate urgency about this small bird's song, a song of hope remarkably cast in the sounds of Sani's reassuring Navajo voice. Topangah enjoys the gentle communion she shares with this bird, a bird Topangah's neighbors to the south, the Kumeyaay, call *Ashaw tu cuk*. She knows she will need Sani's help to uncover its rhapsodic mystery and, albeit very unhurriedly, discover the song's true meaning, for her and for her people. For a long time this small humble bird shares its enchanting melody. "My gift," it sweetly whispers to Topangah, "is my song, and I sing it now for you. It shall be your gift to your people."

Topangah understands gifts are to be received with wonder and humility. She also understands the meaning of song. It is through song we share our origins and relationships. Each song — from the dreaming song, love song, and seeing song, to the traveling song, healing song, and protection song — has a unique purpose, and each is sung exactly as it is taught. For Topangah, singing will become the essence of her world.

Soon, Grandfather Sun rises from the East, where the spirit of fire bathes the canyons in its warm, soothing, yellow light. From this place of beginnings, wisdom walks with the light to provide us the power of knowledge; it is a place of illumination that helps us see things the way they really are, far and wide. Only with this 'beginning' of understanding can the people live good lives.

For Topangah, this first night seemed long waiting for the white dawn. Now well rested and filled with excitement, she must find Sani! Running toward Grandfather Sun's rising, she doesn't have far to go. With his back to the west, he lifts his hands high above the rock altar. Gently rubbing a few willow sticks, smoke visibly rises to Father Sky. A small fire accents Sani's sober expression as he reaches for tobacco and sacred herbs in his *jish*, a small medicine pouch strapped to his side. Lifting his offering to Grandfather Sun, he places it prayerfully on the wings of the wind, first to the east, then south, west, north, up, and down, silently asking Great Spirit for knowledge and understanding. Not only for him, but for all his people, and especially for Topangah during this tumultuous period of discovery that is certain to raise many questions, questions Sani hopes he can help her answer.

"Sani," Topangah speaks softly, not wanting to interrupt what Sani is doing.

Sani quickly replies, "Good morning, Topangah."

"*Yah'ah' teh' ah'bin'eh*, Sani," Topangah says with a beautiful smile.

"How was your run to the east to greet Grandfather Sun and the star nations, and to express your gratitude to Mother Earth this morning?," Sani asks.

Traditionally, children begin their day by giving thanks to Mother Earth for all the gifts of life. They learn at an early age our world is a precious and rare gift; nothing is insignificant. It is easy for most to remember Moon Woman and Grandfather Sun. But there remain other members of the extended 'family' to appreciate, such as small blue flowers in the grassy fields, lone lady bugs, and the rolling rocks and pebbles in our streams. To be thankful is to celebrate the beauty that is Mother Earth.

"Glorious, Sani. It is good to wake before sunrise while the morning star shines brightly in Father Sky. I remember what you have taught me. All things in nature — animals, plants, and the environments that surround them — are interrelated and interact to keep balance with the universe and all its beauty. We are joyfully related — *mitakuye o'yasin* — and I am ever grateful. I lift my voice to Great Spirit with a thankful heart, Sani, for our brothers and sisters on sweet Mother Earth, for our desire to live in peace, for strength and understanding to help us make our world a better place for all, for the lessons hidden along my way, and for future generations."

"What did you want to tell me, Topangah?"

"Sani, I had a dream. Not just any dream."

Dreams have always been regarded with great respect. Dreams are often a source of sacred wisdom and direction for life. From an early age, children are generally encouraged to share their dreams.

"Tell me of this dream, Topangah."

Topangah sat, making sure her skin touched Mother Earth. In this way, she began to feel Mother Earth's healing power through the sacred, soothing, strengthening, and cleansing soil. Topangah knows Mother Earth is full of life and love, always eager to give her powers to those who come to her.

"Sani, I believe it was more like a vision. I was visited by a very small bird. It said it was a good friend of my helper, Eagle. It brought me a beautiful gift, a gift of song."

"Do you remember his song?," Sani asked.

"Yes, Sani. It was a lovely song filled with great respect for Tatanka."

"Only Tatanka, Topangah?"

"No, Sani. A great wind blew from the North, a wise wind that filled me with clarity of mind and spirit. This wind rode a sacred white buffalo. A magnificent black bear from the West shared the same trail with Buffalo. This Bear carried the great waters of rain, rivers, lakes, and springs, great waters without boundary that continually filled my mind, body, soul, and spirit with the strength to shield and protect myself, and others, from harm. A great many buffalo were nearby, most of them young, none as magnificent as the white buffalo, and each welcoming the warmth of Grandfather Sun's rays just peeking from beyond the opposite canyon's rims as he rose into the colorful ribbons of light that laced Father Sky. The breath of the new day made me and my new friends, Bear and the white Buffalo, strong. My spirit and my heart remain filled with love and peace."

"What else can you tell me, Topangah?"

"White Buffalo never left my side, Bear never left her. The remaining buffalo in their midst were watchful, possessing a sweet steadfast anticipation. They were hopeful, Sani. They knew they were where they belonged. But they were not haughty. They seemed unaware of the impact their strong, persistent, and powerful presence might have on others around them. Their respect for life and goodness extended to all life, every creature that swims, flies, walks, and crawls. In welcoming the nurturing and giving nature of Bear, both displayed a kind, generous spirit and an abundant compassion that portrays an uncommon freedom to defend and honor life, all life."

Smiling, Sani nods in approval of what he has heard. After a short interval of reflection, Sani asks, "What have you learned, Topangah?"

"I am reminded, Sani, all living things in nature have their own ritual and ceremony, and each of us are part of a greater whole. We must cultivate a heart of gratitude, thankful for what we have and what we can share with others. We must respect life, all life, if we are to honor the integrity of our own essence. This respect requires a willingness to sacrifice, and to serve. Understanding, acceptance, and joy complete our abundance. Judgment and fear, it seems to me, Sani, cannot stand with respect, an outward manifestation of love."

"Topangah, I am well pleased. Our people have long talked about the legendary powers of Buffalo and Bear. We have become acquainted through stories, prayers, healing practices, songs, ceremonies, and dances. Buffalo teaches us we can stand alone while Bear teaches us we need not do so. Buffalo shares and gives away that we might live. Bear nurtures and cultivates a sense of unearthing within us that we, like the mighty tree, may grow strong."

Sani stops to contemplate another time, perhaps in the days of his youth, as he breathes in the beauty of the mesa. Topangah, rather impatient, reverently asks Sani to continue.

"Each of us must participate in the circle of life, Topangah. The power of the circle always returns to its original starting point. At any one time, some are young, like you, and some, old in years, remain young at heart, like me. Bear represents a coming of age, the maturation from adolescence and youth to adulthood. Buffalo brings to mind our White Hairs, those who have walked the *good red road* for many years. These Elders have come to a time of completion where the wisdom they attained in this life must be shared with others. This 'giveaway' is thorough, and complete. Do you understand, Topangah?"

"Yes, Sani. Please continue."

"Very well, Topangah. The buffalo has always been viewed as another closely related tribe worthy of great respect and admiration. You have, no doubt, heard us speak of a time when Buffalo gave the people everything that was needed. Without Buffalo's help and its sacrifice, the people were as nothing. Buffalo sustained their lives; it was the people's home, their bed, their blanket, their drum, their winter coat, and the flesh of their flesh. Nothing was wasted. Everything was honored and respected. But Tatanka did more than simply meet the physical needs of the people. Many spiritual lessons were to be learned from this great being. There is a story our brothers and sisters to our north tell of a white buffalo calf woman who brings the people hope through the essential nature of spiritual living that restores balance and harmony to our lives. Through White Buffalo Calf Woman, we learn all things are sacred and interconnected. We are one. Everything we do impacts another; it influences everything else. Many fear the responsibility this revelation brings. But you have met Bear, Topangah, who gives us the good courage to stand, alone if needed, and face the truth of White Buffalo Calf Woman's words."

Topangah sits in contemplation, joyfully taking in all Sani has told her. Thinking he is done, she stands. As she does, Sani adds, "Topangah, Buffalo understands what it means to serve and to sacrifice out of a deep respect for all living things. Your friend, Eagle, teaches us only those who possess the courage love demands can stand without fear, free and in harmony with nature, as they create authentic, long-lasting relations that are a true expression of respect. Such a love courageously stands face to face against the winds of adversity to see the good in all things."

For some time, Topangah and Sani enjoyed the company of a quiet solitude. With a joyful heart, Topangah soon lifts her voice to Above World.

"O' Great Spirit," Topangah spoke, "there are so many needs. I have many desires. Whereupon the path of this life I choose to serve many depend. Fear and limitations slow down my progress. Balance is needed. Open my heart as well as my eyes today as I ask but for one thing. Please guide me with the teachings of the people and help me overcome my fear that I might experience love, a genuine, enduring love for others with a connection so strong it prevails over any boundaries that might get in the way of me serving others in this world. From my eyes, tears freely flow like a raging river down my cheek. Yet I am unafraid to experience my fear and turn in the direction of the noble life I have been searching for; only then, I know, will I come face to face with the fearlessness I seek."

"O' Great Spirit, thank you for the four sacred mountains that welcome me home, and thank you for Father Sky whose reach, like the depth of love, goes on forever."

"O' Great Spirit, I will do what it takes to open my heart to the needs of others, to escape any tendency to judge, to cast no stone. Through the power of the love you share with me, I shall find the daring I need to help our people overcome and, with the power of a prairie wind, return, like Buffalo, to make the land whole again, saving ourselves so we, too, may one day have the courage to dance."

3

Courage: Dance with the Bear ~ Behold the Beauty Within

A bear lifted me up so I could see all the earth.
Full Mouth (Crow)

Topangah devoted much of her morning and the sun-shines to reverent thoughts of Tatanka before unexpectedly turning her heart and mind to Great Bear from the west, the devoted friend who, with a glad heart, walked the same trail with Tatanka. She knew something important was taking place, but what it was and, more importantly, what it means for her and her people remained elusive. Uncertain where to begin, Topangah searched for the nuances that make all things beautiful. Most lives are lived, she mused, in some semblance of mediocrity while others, like Tatanka, possess vastly deeper meaning, made noble through the enduring and indefatigable relationship of a indisputable friend.

"That's it," Topangah thought to herself, not knowing her thoughts were more like gentle whispers that carried softly to Sani's ear. "Tatanka and Bear share more than the same trail. Great Bear sees Tatanka first as his friend."

Saying nothing, Sani listens on as Topangah unknowingly reasons aloud. "Friendship is a choice one makes that does not necessarily depend on the other," Topangah adds. "When I see how the small birch grows under the protection of large pines, I come to know the authentic nature of a deep abiding friendship. Both the birch and the pine desperately need sunlight to survive, yet they have resolved themselves to share the same space in recognition — and celebration — of their diversity. They 'see' each other as friends that can help one another, not adversaries. The message is clear; it's one of love."

"Sani?"

"Yes, Topangah."

"What do you know of friendship?," Topangah asks.

"I know it takes courage to stand with your friend," Sani softly answers before adding, "I also know the decision as to whether another is accepted as your friend belongs to you, not to them. In my younger years, I often heard my Navajo grandfathers sing and chant about the importance of friendship, their familiar words warmly, confidently carried by whispering winds to hearts everywhere. I can hear them just now,

> 'I have been to the end of the Earth.
> I have been to the end of the waters.
> I have been to the end of the sky.
> I have been to the end of the mountains.
> I have found none that are not my friends.'"

"What does it mean, Sani?"

"It means the only way to wake up with enemies is to refuse to accept them as friends. We are not confined, after all, to *their* definition of the relationship."

"Is that why it takes courage to stand with a friend, Sani?"

"Yes, Topangah. And, no. Bravery certainly can be an outward expression of our courage. But the strength of character that endures comes from a conviction that invites us to stand in stillness, and wait, often alone at some of our most vulnerable moments. In our stillness, we gain insight. Like Tatanka, who resolutely stands in some of the deepest snows with his head facing the fiercest winds, our courage can manifest itself in our own determination to stand shoulder to shoulder with a friend, come what may. But courage is also necessary — perhaps, more so — if we are to find the requisite strength to stand our ground with integrity and confront our greatest enemy. Do you know this most menacing foe, Topangah?"

"I only know it saddens me deeply to realize I have an enemy, Sani. Who is it?"

With that question, Sani momentarily loses himself in profound thought. After all, Topangah knows only to see with her heart. Such a view of the world can only help her when the time comes to take steps to become the people's singer — their spiritual teacher, healer, and leader. Steps sure to include certain trials and tests, dreams, vision quests, her calling, the many years of training in patience and understanding she will receive as an apprentice, and the discipline of her mind, body, emotions, soul, and spirit.

"That enemy, Topangah, is the same enemy each of us must confront; without fanfare, it patiently lies in wait within. You see, Topangah, my greatest enemy is myself. Fortunately, the same holds true for you. There's nothing to fear; quite to the contrary, there is much to learn in facing our greatest foe, facing our fears, and facing the difficulties life has strewn along our path. For most, it is a very easy task to deflect responsibility; few there are who understand it takes great courage to accept it. In so accepting, we choose to judge no one but ourselves as we do our small part to further another's journey. Like you, Topangah, each person must overcome unique challenges and obstacles to climb their own mountain. Think of Bear, he who walks with Tatanka. In the safe retreat of his den, he has many moons for self reflection, to seek wisdom through stillness and meditation, and to look deep within him. Who, but himself, is there to assign blame or appoint fault? Tatanka's friend, Great Bear, teaches us to awaken the courage that lies dormant and bravely look within. Looking within, we learn to do what is right. We learn to heal that which is not well within us. We learn to transform our fears into action that gives rise to a good life."

With Grandfather Sun standing high in the vast deep blue recesses of Father Sky, Topangah needs some time to absorb all Sani has shared with her. She takes a short walk. For reasons that will become clearer, her short excursion begins and ends thinking of buffalo calves, especially those separated from their mothers through illness or, perhaps, death. In fear and confusion those calves instinctively stand in a tight formation, still as a small bird in the presence of a soaring Peregrine falcon. Once free of the fear, their tender grunts and frolicking are interrupted only by the occasional sniffing of this and that, or a tasty meal of sweetgrass. Having separated themselves from their fear, they soon experience love and begin to welcome precious moments of play, swinging and lowering their wooly heads and kicking up their heels among a tangle of sagebrush, prairie grass, rabbitbrush — a plant that can dye wool as bright as Grandfather Sun! — and the iridescent rust of bluestem as they paw the ground before aiming their short, ebony horn buds at a neighboring calf. With sudden bursts of furry energy, they charge with unrelenting joy, a joy that finds its way back to Topangah. Her thoughts of playful hooves splashing across green grassy fields find company with a long-awaited smile, and a burning desire to learn more.

Topangah's return is welcomed by Sani's soft voice asking if she recalls her earlier question, 'If we leave, how can we always be close by?'

How strange it is, Topangah thinks, that Sani would bring up that specific discussion just after devoting much of her early afternoon to think of young buffalo that have lost their mothers.

"I remember, Sani," Topangah replied. "Can you help me understand?," she implores.

"Of course," Sani begins. "As we walk the path before us, in and out of lives, let us learn from Great Bear's slow ambling gait to bravely and purposefully bring new life — a kind of spring medicine that does not isolate but connects — with the healing power of love to lay upon the wounds of our people. Let us send up a sacred smoke that tenderly touches creation — our Relations, how we live our lives, and our feelings of wholeness and belonging. Let us, like our friend, Bear, look out among the stars to find our way."

As Topangah quietly listens, Sani continues, "Our life of service, Topangah, most certainly and ever so silently becomes our gift, a gift of great worth, not unlike Buffalo draped in the white winter solitude of the North. Upon acceptance, our gift finds it way deep into the hearts of those who, like Grandfather Sun, dance with us, as well as those who rise another morning to dance after us."

In deep contemplation, Topangah remains silent.

Hearing nothing from Topangah, Sani adds, "Our gift, not unlike Grandfather Sun's gift, covers a great distance and, in its stillness and solitude, it always gives back. It has no other purpose. In living our lives as gifts for another, the people see us approaching even when the path we walk lies beyond the horizon. Because time and space can no longer separate us, we can never be far away. In our giving, Topangah, we are always nearby. And in our leaving, our gift keeps us close, as if it finds a place in the hearts of those we leave behind to draw life — and other gifts — from all who walk under the warm light of Grandfather Sun."

"Sani?"

"Yes, Topangah."

"Does Great Bear walk with Tatanka so he can leave something behind?"

"It's more than that, Topangah," Sani tells her. "Great Bear, like Tatanka, is very important to our people. So much so, we celebrate their teachings in our dances, our ceremonies, our stories, our songs, and everyday life. From Tatanka, we learn to stand alone, if necessary, and to share and give away. From Great Bear, we learn to nurture and cultivate a healthy sense of who we are; we come to understand how important it is to discover our path and to find our place among our people."

Sani pauses to allow Topangah to grasp all he has said because the most important words are yet to come.

"Topangah, listen carefully."

"I am, Sani," Topangah interjects not knowing there was no need to do so.

"Together, Tatanka and Great Bear help us to restore harmony and to keep life in balance amid change. They remind us of the circle of life, and the importance of renewal and fresh beginnings. Their medicine heals not just our life, but the life of our people, the life of the community we share, the life of our Relations, and the life of our friends, even if some might see those same friends as enemies. The courage we seek is a gift from Great Bear that helps us heal our world."

Giving Topangah time to ponder the meaning of his words, Sani asks, "How would you describe Great Bear, Topangah?"

"Like Tatanka, Sani, I sense Great Bear is everywhere — and nowhere — at the same time. He not only chooses to be Tatanka's friend, but he is my friend, too. I can feel his presence before me at this moment. He possesses a fearless energy. No. I think it is more like unbounded love. There is a gentle strength about him, Sani, that is powerful, yet open to potential. He is large, and strong. His all-embracing love equips me with the courage to turn away fear, to look deep within, and to discover my true self so I may reach out with unbridled compassion and a helping hand to aid others in similar discoveries of their own."

"You have learned much, Topangah."

Topangah reflects on Sani's teachings and, more importantly, his love for her and their people.

After a short time, Sani speaks. "There's more, Topangah. Let's walk."

With that offer, they turn to the west.

In that very moment, Topangah spies her friend, Eagle, high above the buttes and ridge tops. She thinks about the love it takes to be courageous, and the courage it takes to love.

Sani sees Eagle, too.

"Eagle, Topangah, does not ask our consent to exist. He simply is. And he is intimately aware of what he is and what he can do for others. Like you and me, he draws strength, conviction, and vision from Great Bear."

"What do you mean, Sani?"

"Bear gives life to the land. It is chiefly a Mother symbol that provides many lessons in the way it lives. Among other things, it helps us better understand how we act, think, and interact. Great Bear is the spirit keeper of the West, a dark, mysterious place of maturity where observation, introspection, change, dreams, and visions provide a good harvest. Bear teaches the importance of independent thinking necessary to unravel problems and bring about healing. He teaches us to seek peace in quiet meditation so we may learn to trust our awakened intuition and listen to our inner voice. Through meditation, dreams, and visions, he helps us seek knowledge. Like Eagle, he teaches us to simply *be*. With this self-awareness, we find a kind of blind, powerful surge of courage in our mental and moral strength to overcome any fear that prevents us from living our true spirit with profound meaning that moves our people forward with a renewed sense of direction, action, and wisdom."

Sani stops briefly. Topangah uses the time to reflect.

"Great Bear," Sani reports, "is our guide to the deep river of awareness and meaning where our people can rediscover who they are and what they stand for, and remember their way. He teaches us to have a strong heart, and to respond to pain and suffering, all pain and suffering, with compassion so we might better help others embark on their journey, a journey bringing them closer to the meaning of what they have done and what remains for them to do. We do not stand alone, just as Tatanka need not stand alone. Even here among the desert sands and majestic mesas, we are joined by coyotes, bobcats, wild turkeys, songbirds, rabbits, rats, mice, and porcupine. Ravens, hawks, and our friend, Eagle, soar above. An important part of courage is knowing when we are needed, and stepping forward when the time is right. It is with this newfound courage to create shared meaning, a gift from Bear, we save ourselves. You see, Topangah, Bear gives us power and strength not only to be, but to love."

Sani's words, though short, are full of truth, and speak volumes on the meaning of life and the joy of living courageously. Topangah already has learned much this day, and she earnestly wishes to discover deeper truths. She takes a moment to ask Great Spirit to share in her delight.

"O' Great Spirit, thank you for the majesty, freedom, and power of our Brother, Great Bear. Thank you for teaching us our Brother is a symbol of what is right with our world; he reminds us to do what is right even if it is unpopular, or the consequences are unpleasant. Thank you for his incredible influence, and the wisdom he imparts."

"O' Great Spirit, thank you for Bear's watchfulness that encourages us to discern man's intent. Thank you for Bear's fierce spirit and the bravery we muster when we think upon our Brother. Thank you for Bear's power and the conviction it nurtures within a strong heart. Thank you for our Brother's yearning for peace, and his call for harmony and balance."

"O' Great Spirit, thank you for Bear Brother's life. I am comforted knowing Bear is my friend. Thank you that my Brother and I are made of the same dust, breathe the same winds, and drink from the same waters. Thank you that my Brother and I are warmed by Grandfather Sun, and joyfully abide under Father Sky's slate-blue canopy. Thank you that my Brother and I enjoy a life made all the more joyful with every valley, every plain and grove, and every shadow Grandfather Sun walks across our Earth Mother. Thank you that my Brother and I merely need to ask for the better, deeper, and wider blessing the grandfathers hold in store for us. Thank you that my Brother and I can discover the mysteries that lie within our heart that you would have us behold."

"O' Great Spirit, thank you that Bear Brother lives on, as does the beauty of all living things before me, behind me, above me, below me, and all around me."

4

Honesty: Walk Your Talk with Good Judgment and the Gentleness of a 'Great Elder Brother'

Honesty comes when you learn to be fearless with yourself. When you speak and act straight from the heart, the Creator will give you love and strength to say and do what is right for you in every moment. Innocence, curiosity, and openness will keep you honest.
~Goyathlay (Geronimo), Chiricahua Apache chief

The copper-red, rugged sandstone mesas and bluffs rising abruptly out of the desert plain reflect an innate beauty that is both fundamentally nourishing and uniquely inspiring. In their midst, among the deep canyons, shallow washes, low basins, valley oases, and dry, windblown river beds, one can find a deep, abiding power for the people, the *Diné* as Sani often says, to believe in themselves and to be strong. Radiating a sense of harmony, balance, and wellness, the natural presence of light and warmth nurtures and cultivates a sacredness about life and living that brings about healing and growth. Everything here affects everything else. Sani knows this. Sani also knows the respect and honor of relationship is at the heart of this harmony, balance, and wellness. Earth, wind, and water combine with mind, body, and spirit to bring about what Sani's people refer to as hózhó *náhásdlíí*, walking in beauty. To walk in beauty is to be in balance with the universe, to insure harmony and joy continue for all.

"All roads are good," Sani remarks, catching Topangah by surprise. "Everything — and everyone — matters. Deep canyons are no less important than majestic mountains. The wind is just as vital as the rain. Those who follow are in no way inferior to those who would lead them. The servant is no less needed than those they serve. Greatness is all around us, Topangah. It recognizes and understands we are equal to others — to all relations — but not better, that there is no proper place for position, prominence, or power. Seeds of greatness are drawn from humility and service."

Topangah took to heart Sani's words before asking, "What is greatness?"

"Greatness is the prerogative of the people, Topangah, perfected in humility, service, and love."

"Why is love so important, Sani?"

"There is a story of kindness and generosity in each of us, Topangah, a story of love. I suppose that's because love is the power of the people; it's what we are. When it comes to singing, healing, spiritual teaching, and leading, the nature of love is such that singers, healers, teachers, and leaders serve first, sing, heal, teach, and lead second. A true leader clearly understands they cannot effectively lead until they first learn how to love because it is not leaders the people seek; they seek to know love. The gift of leadership is love. Said differently, Topangah, the power of the love shared between followers and those they choose to lead them is the only thing that gives rise to leadership. That is to say, love brings leadership to life."

A brief silence left Topangah with an important question to ask, "Can any leader love, Sani?"

"Yes, Topangah, any leader can love. Many do. It's simply concealed in a tough exterior that builds walls around any emotion that might escape. Some leaders make the conscious choice not to love, at least openly, for reasons they, themselves, likely do not fully understand or, in some cases, are unwilling to face."

"Why would a leader not jump at the opportunity to demonstrate their love for those they lead, Sani?"

Sani thought for a while as Grandfather Sun began to hang lower in Father Sky.

"Our tendency, Topangah, especially as leaders, is to complicate our simple lives with unnecessary clutter; anything to distract us and detach us from the fear which, for many, rages within. A leader who has no love for those they serve lacks the consummate courage to look beyond the fear they hold within. You see, Topangah, fear rages because it has not been set free. Only in facing our fear head on can faith find room to draw near, giving a leader the courage to take a stand, even if they must stand alone. You see, Topangah, we are put in this world not to be better than the next man but rather help him be better than he was when we met. We must not overlook the little things we can do for another. Although a puff of wind can move a giant boulder if the time is right, no suitable place exists among the people for one to overpower another. Instead," Sani adds, "respect and empowerment help us acknowledge and value others. The leader who puts the people before self will not judge; instead, their grace, strength, and wisdom will seek to understand the thoughts, fears, and curiosities of those who have chosen them to lead. Together, they can pierce any darkness with the compassionate light of love. That's because love gently nudges us but in one direction: to continually look for the good in others. Do you know why, Topangah?," Sani asks.

"It seems to me the right thing to do, Sani," Topangah offered.

"Perhaps, Topangah, but I think it's simpler than that. Love nudges us to look for the good in others because we are certain to find it! Isn't that what it means to sing, heal, teach, and lead? Those who would lead must have community support; they must be embraced by the people if they are to become a servant to the people. Have you ever noticed how trees reach out and touch one another as they grow, Topangah? Or how the flowers dance and gracefully accept the kisses of the wind? It is the same for us; we are to reach out to others, to touch them so all of us can grow."

Both pause to think of the people, and to recount their many varied needs. For Topangah, it is a coming home moment. Like the smell of piñon smoke drifting through the high desert air heralds a season of change, Sani's words magically transport Topangah to a new place of understanding, really a place of remembrance, that helps her honor and respect the ways of her people, a generous and giving people whose prayerful songs, like dancing flames, pass over, around, and through so many. With each new song, a mystical, even mysterious, beauty finds its way above, below, behind, and in front of all who pass this way.

As the time of sun-shines slips silently into early eve', a flash of lightening draws Topangah's attention to great billowing thunderheads building in the south. The sky will soon fill with the howl of the winds and the sudden crash of thunder that echoes through deep narrow canyons. Just as abruptly, Topangah knows the air will thicken as it becomes still and silent before another rush of wind, thunder, and lightning announces the arrival of a magnificent downpour. With certainty, small drops of water will soon give way to a silver-gray curtain of rain. Only a few minutes will pass before the roar of rushing streams can be heard from the canyon's dry river beds far below. In the same moment, dark clouds will blow away making room for Grandfather Sun to preside over a dripping, steamy world. In those few precious minutes, pools will fill with fresh water and springs, once dormant, shall burst to life. As the rain comes to an end, clouds rise to take their place in a long parade of natural elements, content to race shadows across the face of Mother Earth. Topangah turns to Sani, expecting to ask a question but, instead, quietly sits, certain wonderful things are in the making.

She closes her eyes to more fully contemplate life among the people of *Dinétah*. They know the land that sits within the boundaries of their four sacred mountains, Those-Who-Stand-Under-The-Sky. The spiritual beings know the *Diné*. Topangah has often heard Sani remind the people the mesa tops, red buttes, and towering spires of red, russet, and brown sandstone rising from the flat desert valley of standing rocks are the stepping stones the gods use when they walk the earth. The people speak with great respect for Bear and Rabbit, Right Mitten, Left Mitten, Three Sisters, the King and His Throne, Elephant Butte, Black Rock Canyon, Canyon del Muerto, Canyon de Chelly, Monument Canyon, Eagle Mesa, and Spider Rock. Everything around them lives!

Among her people, Topangah has learned she, like all other daughters, is to learn the responsibilities of home from Amá, her mother, while it is customary for a young man of her age to spend a great deal of time with a ceremonial father, someone who helps him learn the legends, rituals, songs, and chants he will perform in life's later ceremonial work. Of course, many of these young men earnestly yearn for the treasured and privileged learning that comes by sitting, even for scores of years, at the feet of *hataalii* — their healer and spiritual teacher, the medicine man. Sani, well aware of Topangah's gifts, takes the time to speak aloud of tradition, stating, "Medicine, Topangah, refers to those things that bring us closer to nature, to the life force resident in all living things. In many ways, we are medicine for one another; the medicine man and medicine woman, however, are held in highest esteem, great respect, and honor among their people. They know — and understand — the old ways, the heritage and culture, and history, legends, and myths of their people. The medicine man preserves the traditions and beliefs of his people; in many ways, he is the holder of truth about his people's way of life. The medicine man walks the Beauty Way; he tells the young and reminds the old balance and harmony with all living things is very important to one's own well-being. The medicine man has spent many hours learning songs and prayers that he will someday teach to a very special young man who will eventually take his place among the people."

Of course, there are times, Sani has wisely learned, when it is better if the young man, well, isn't a man at all. Now is such a time, for in their midst a special young maiden stands out, somehow destined to lead her people. Where-Mountain-Meets-The-Sea, Sani has instructed his people, is such a maiden. And Sani silently delights in his role as Topangah's ceremonial father.

Without Topangah's noticing, Sani has tied a blue sash around his head, and is just now gracefully placing several bundles of cloth on a narrow flat rock along the high wall's edge protected by the sheltered cliffside. Not yet fully aware of all that is going on, Topangah nervously sits with wide-eyed anticipation as Sani unrolls the bundles to reveal beautiful eagle feathers tied together with a strip of leather, and a small leather pouch, his medicine bundle. A small bowl of sacred water, Topangah notices, already sits on the rock.

"Topangah, this *jish* once belonged to my grandfather. It is a strong medicine bundle containing soil from each of the four sacred mountains: *Tsisna'jini* to the East, *Tsoodzil* to the South, *Doko'oosliid* to the West, and *Dibé Ntsaa* to the North. There remain two other mountains you need to know. The first, All Creation (Rainbow) Mountain, provides a sacred door for spiritual work, and Medicine Mountain, the second, is home to many healing herbs. Three important rivers also make their home here: the Rio Grande, the Colorado, and the San Juan."

Sani takes some time to explain to Topangah Navajos believe they were originally placed on the land between the four sacred mountains, representing the four cardinal directions. Tsisna'jini, Dawn or White Shell Mountain, is what later becomes known as Blanca Peak near Alamosa in San Luis Valley, Colorado. Tsoodzil, Blue Bead or Turquoise Mountain, is later named Mount Taylor, north of Laguna, New Mexico. Doko'oosliid, Abalone Shell Mountain, is anointed Francisco Peak near Flagstaff, Arizona. And Dibé Ntsaa, Big Mountain Sheep or Obsidian Mountain, is later referred to as Hesperus Peak in the La Plata Mountains of Colorado.

Without as much as a single word, Sani turns toward Topangah. Waving and twirling eagle feathers over

Topangah, Sani sprinkles her as his repetitive, rhythmic, atonal voice resonates over the mesa. Sani's chant is familiar to Topangah. She recalls hearing his blessing ceremony, complete with glottal stops that resonate deep inside, many times. It is good medicine, both magical and powerful, with a calming effect that brings balance and restores harmony across the mesa, and as far as the eyes can see. Sani's blessing is largely a way to communicate with the natural world — Topangah's growing world — their love and respect for every living thing. The *Diné* are not alone in their belief all living things share the same father (Sun) and mother (Earth) and, as such, we are related. From the voice of the thunder behind a dark cloud to the voice of the smallest insect playing among tender plants, Sani knows Topangah is learning how everything is connected; how every animal and every environment, like every person, has a spirit and a life of its own that is beautiful and should be respected. In blessing Topangah, as well as this mesa and all life upon it, Sani demonstrates the importance of leading by example. This Topangah understands, having enjoyed the rare opportunity these last several years to watch an authentic leader's 'walk' do the talking for him.

"Sani," Topangah begins, "what must I learn to lead the people?"

"There is, of course, much to learn Topangah, but you can begin by learning what nature and the elements — wind, rain, mountains, corn, and clouds — want to teach you this day."

Topangah thought deeply for a moment. "Sani, do they not teach to heal and help one another?," Topangah shyly asks.

"Yes, Topangah. But there is more. We first learn from nature and the elements to possess a strong faith in who we are, and to possess the courage to be true to our self so others will have faith in us. Only then is it possible for us to serve their needs with healing and growth."

"How can I become like the wind, the rain, and Grandfather Sun, Sani?"

"Trust yourself, Topangah, and ask Great Spirit to guide you. Consider Eagle. It is in his oneness with the wind that we learn to cultivate and nurture the love so very necessary for healing and growth. Drawing unto the people requires us to let go of who we are so we may become who it is we were meant to be. I hope you understand, Topangah."

"I'm beginning to, Sani."

"Now is the time, Topangah, for you to be honest with yourself, to be true to yourself, to accept yourself for who you are, to practice a strong sense of respect for and confidence in your self, and to walk without shame so you may more easily make room for who you may become. In this way, you find the will and determination to lovingly serve others and help them become who it is they are meant to be. Does not the sun gently warm both the mighty mountain and the babbling brook expecting nothing in return? Does not the summer rain fall sweetly upon all, both the *Diné* and every other nation — red, yellow, white, and black? And does the rain not become one with Mother Earth and Father Sky? The lesson, Topangah, is this: when you speak, speak truthfully. There will soon come a time when the people will need you, and they will need to know you are there to serve them. Be ready for that time. Grow your gift so you might take the people right into the stories you tell. Remember, you will not need so many words, only powerful words. Those words, coupled with your gentle manner, will bring sacred thoughts and truths to life for the people. They will come to see what it is you see. Sit with me, Topangah. I will tell you a story."

"Among the peoples of the Plains to the north, specifically the Lakotah, and among their brothers further north, there is a being of flesh and spirit regarded with great respect, a being that loves as any humbled people might love. He goes by many names, for many nations know him: some call him Sabe, Saape, and Sasquatch. The Navajo call him *Yé'iitsoh*, or Big God, while our Lakotah brothers prefer to call him, *Chiye-Tanka* — Great Elder Brother. He is seen as a kind of special being with a special kind of power. A simple touch from *Chiye-Tanka* is as a blessing held in highest regard by the people. Ever-waiting and ever-present, he lives alone in wild places, always honest, and always content to gather with no other. *Chiye-Tanka* has always loved the land to which he belongs. His passion, dedication, intelligence, and wisdom enable him to fight long and hard — even today — to heal the wounds of Mother Earth, to protect balance and harmony among his many relations, and to help humanity overcome our misguided ambitions and the ill effects of selfishness and greed. As humans continue to willingly harm one another and wantonly destroy the environment, *Chiye-Tanka* has the courage to stand for truth, making us utterly aware of the consequences of negating justice — and conscience — in favor of expediency, and reminding us of our kinship with other forms of life, even as he, himself, struggles like many of us for a bare decent life, the well-being of his children, and the survival of his peoples. If we are to be at peace with nature, he would tell us, we must first be at peace with ourselves. *Chiye-Tanka* walks in beauty to bring our lands the respect it deserves so our homes will have some meaning for our children and our children's children."

As *Chiye-Tanka* watches over sacred spaces, it is his prerogative to remind us when we have upset the balance and harmony of our existence. Like a brother who looks out for us, he maintains a close relationship with all living things: he is one with humanity, the animals, the rivers, the plants, the elements, and the stars. To him, we are closely related, a family. With utmost care, he gently urges us to restore good judgment and regain our once strong respect for all creatures, great and small. The spiritual nature of this gentle beast gives him a familiar power common to all; the power to love, like a brother. From the wanderings of our Elder Brother, a great and sacred animal who walks among the *Diné*, we learn, more from his power and his dilemma than anything else, what he has set out to teach us: to be honest to the natural laws of creation and to each other, to embrace an uncommon humility, and to be one with the people."

"Sani, please tell me story and life come together as one. I want so very much to meet my great elder brother. Can I see *Chiye-Tanka?*," Topangah innocently asks.

"In many ways, Topangah, you already do. Because there are many paths to perfection, one must only look with new eyes to see. Like the wind that carries the soaring eagle higher and higher into the sky, *Chiye-Tanka's* love, ever-present within our midst, freely carries us deeper and deeper into one another's hearts. In choosing to see each other as fellow beings, sojourners as it were, we give them room to express their humanity. In this way, we give the people their wings to fly."

For what seems a long time, both Topangah and Sani contemplate the magnitude of *Chiye-Tanka's* great capacity for love and compassion as a leader — a great elder brother — to the people. Topangah seizes upon her thoughts with a whispered prayer.

"O' Great Spirit, may those things said of our Great Elder Brother be said about us: 'There walks an honest being that keeps his promises and can be trusted.' I ask you to bring to life the teachings of our Elders, helping us to 'never try to be someone else.' Help us live true to our spirit. Help us to be honest to our self. Help us to accept who we are, the way you made us."

"O' Great Spirit, let us walk tall like *Chiye-Tanka*, our Great Elder Brother who seeks no fame or glory. And let us, like him, seek not the prominence, power, speed, or beauty of another. *Chiye-Tanka* wants no more than he has been given; it is enough for him, and it is enough for us."

"Help us, O' Great Spirit, to pass through the high mesas and deep canyons of life without leaving a trace of our presence behind. Let us possess an uncommon humility."

5
Humility: Embrace the Heart of the Wolf ~ Submit Yourself to the Greater Good

We all walk this Good Earth Road as creatures of the One Creator. The rising and falling of the Sun each day, the seasons, the gifts of food, shelter, love, and friendship are there for each of us in the One Circle. If you cannot find the way to be grateful in your heart, the fault lies within you.
~ Tecumthe, Chief Tecumseh (Crouching Tiger), Shawnee

Topangah woke thinking, "They love as any humbled people might love." Then she asked herself aloud, "Who loves as any humbled people might love?"

Then she recalled Sani's story of the *Chiye-Tanka*.

"Was it just a dream?" she asked herself. It felt so real, so very essential. She knew dreams can connect us, as an extension of daily living, to a world greater than ourselves. They tell us things. They make us wonder. They help us understand. Only, on this occasion, something, or someone, was missing, but she knew not why. The details are slow in coming to her. It's no wonder. Night can fall cold on the mesa and, as darkness closed around them, she recalled a most delightful conversation with Sani, a conversation she remembered well. She also remembered the light of Moon Woman casting a warm glow and an abiding brightness over the red land. Amidst the beauty of a autumn's evening sky, Topangah was left wondering, "Why *Chiye-Tanka*? And, why now?" Perhaps time would tell.

Fading-time, as she recalled, began with a meal of warm mush made from parched and winnowed piñon nuts. As Topangah's senses drew her closer to the rich, ethereal, cedar-like aroma rising from the fire, she could not help but compare Sani's skills to those of her grandmother. For the uninitiated, piñon nuts are typically ground into flour and used for breads and soups, or mush seasoned with marrow fat. Maize, beans, or squash are usually served with the meal. From time to time, grandmother's mush included tasty plants such as cattails, wolfberry, buckberry, sweet chokecherries, acorns, agave, camas, sego lily, tobacco root, yampa, biscuitroot, bitterroot, and mesquite. This night, Topangah and Sani enjoyed *wojapi* — berry soup — and fry bread with their mush, warmed to perfection by placing hot stones in a basket containing the mush until it was ready to serve. When winter arrives, the same mush might be placed outside to create a frozen treat!

With full — and warm — stomachs, Sani and Topangah sat with grateful hearts in quiet solitude. Out of the silence, Sani's poignant words rise to meet Father Sky like sparks from the evening fire carried proudly skyward to Above World. Sani recalls a distant time, a time of great sorrow when his own grandfather released the deep sadness in his heart with the fall of a single tear that gently traced an aged trail down his weathered cheek, followed by no other, ever. With the reflection of Moon Woman's sky lake (some say night-sun while others speak only of a full moon) shining solemnly against the tears gathering in Sani's own eyes, Sani softly whispers, "Too much of the past has perished and passed beyond our reach." Taking another moment to reflect, he added, "Only winter can lead to spring."

Against the black of night, the distant canyon walls appeared to be bathed in the bright rays of a golden falling-leaves-moon as low-hung stars scattered across the dark quilted sky kept an attentive watch over the mesa. Not knowing exactly what to say, Topangah began, "Sani, I have heard some say spring has come, that the flowers of a new springtime are beginning to open their gentle petals to a soft, growing light of awareness. And I hear them tell others to look past the obvious, a façade that is little more than an illusion really, to that which lies deep within. Only then will we come to know Grandfather Sun and Mother Earth have bounty — and beauty — enough for all. Although we may not fully understand how it will all happen, they invite us to experience and share the love they have come to know. They say each of us has a special beauty that comes to us as we embrace and embody our *knowing*. To each, they say, is granted the power to give life, or destroy it. The decision, of course, has always been ours. It is, they say, only a wise choice — the peaceful way — that heralds a new spring. Such is the choice they have made. Because time flows without bounds, maybe winter *has* passed, Sani, even if we sit here this night under the glow of a falling-leaves-moon."

Sani, a man of great warmth, depth, humor, and compassion, is a bit surprised at Topangah's remark. He did not realize he had spoken aloud, nor did it occur to him that

Topangah had heard his words. But he was glad she did. "Topangah, I have seen many winters pass into spring. Though you have seen far fewer, we walk the same road and we struggle in the same cause, only at different points in time that profoundly shape our perceptions. Yet, both of us lose ourselves in the beauty that colors our world. My journey now nears an end while yours is yet to begin. With much intuition, grace, respect, and humility, we must look forward to all that follows. Indeed, we must look with great expectation to a new spring as winter comes and goes her way."

For Topangah, it was not so much what Sani said that made him a teacher; it was what he did. She was able to learn by simply observing him. He belonged here, and she knew her place was where she found him. "From you, Sani, I have learned life is not a world of neat and linear sequences tied to cause and effect, moving from past to future; nor is it framed with a beginning and an end. Instead, it is intricate and round, like this world, both circular and overlapping with nothing to fear. It is a place where everything finally seeks to become a part of the original oneness. As the seasons change, the sun always moves in the same direction, the stars rise in the same pattern to find their place as they travel the night's sky, and birth gives rise to the certainty of death. The circle symbolizes balance, unity, and renewal. Ours is a journey through time and space that does not end where the circle began, yet it brings us back to our destiny. Ours is a shared destiny, isn't it?"

"Topangah, each of us have our destiny. Mine is here with you. For a time. You see, Topangah, we need to be in the moment if we are to respond to each occasion with the truth that comes from the core of who we are. Because our cores are connected, we share many of the same moments. We have only to look to the four directions. The four directions surround us and keep us going; they bring balance to our lives. All directions are sacred, but only because of each other. From every corner of our world, we see the homes of a peaceful people, each with a beautiful life way, and each with a will to endure the tests of time, however difficult or tragic. Their teachings are timeless. Like others around us, ours is an intimate connection with a world that rises from a passionate need to embrace and experience all that shapes life — plants, animals, rocks, birds, environments, and the elements (earth, wind, water, and fire) — and absorb something of their teachings."

"What must come from these teachings, Sani?"

That Topangah could not yet fully understand was unimportant; it was enough for her to feel at ease among her many friends — her many brothers and sisters that share the same circle of life. Sani would bring it all into focus soon enough. "Topangah, recall the silence you heard at the beginning of our journey? If we surround ourselves with an unusual stillness, a total silence, while in the company of nature, the teachers — and the teachings — we seek find us. Theirs is a collective voice that bridges the past with a perfect and complete future. The only thing required of us is to stay acutely aware."

With only a moment's pause, Sani continues, "Through their voices, we soon learn all that lives, every brother — the eight-legged, the six, the four, and the two-legged ones, the winged-ones, green-growing beings, those that swim and those that crawl — dances in the circle of life. Each depends on another and all are to be respected. Let us not forget some must die before their time because life must be taken so others may live. The grasshopper and the plants that sustain him have been crushed. Fish have been removed from the water. Birds have been taken from the sky. Deer and Buffalo have given of themselves so others may live. So it is those who have taken that they might live must, in its own turn, give back so the circle of life is never broken. It is only when we completely embrace this awareness of life as a circle with hearts that hold no doubt and face this world without fear that we learn humility and find balance. Our humility and our humanity seek common good. All beings are equal, not better than another; the wind blows without preference into all the corners of the world. As part of a great circle, all creation (every stone, plant, and animal) is needed to complete the whole. The silence that now becomes a frequent and welcomed friend also comes together to help heal the past and bring beauty to the present. It is a moment at once awesome and wonderful. With this awareness come humility and the gift of harmony.

Sani's words were full of meaning from which Topangah drank hope. After some time, she asked, "What does humility require?"

Sani should have expected Topangah's question. Maybe he did. "Topangah, Mother Earth and Father Sky provide for us, but they also challenge us. Humanity, after all, is not above creation, only a part of it. We must forge a respectful, balanced relationship with the world around us and seek the harmonious unity of all forms of life. We cannot ignore life's songs; they rise like a magnificent opus from our hearts. As the harmonic voices of birdsong, the great breathing mountains, the song of another's heart, and the song of life rise out of the depths in long, clear tones to become one, the song — our song — grows louder. You see, Topangah, we do not choose to be a singer, a healer, a spiritual teacher, or a leader. We assume a leadership role, not because we have chosen such a position, but because that leadership role has chosen us. We have been chosen because we listen. We have been chosen because we help others say what needs to be said. We paint their words on the ground in the colors of Mother Earth. Because we stand between worlds, we can feel the wonder of it all. We can see and hear what others dare not dream. Yet, humility requires us to embrace what we know without needing to know everything. It requires us to look at ourselves only with the intention of truly knowing ourselves."

"What more can you tell me about humility, Sani?"

"Topangah, humility affirms the inherent worth of all creatures, great and small, by placing the needs of others before ourselves. It requires us to call out our message of hope; share it with all people and all living things on the Mother Earth. Humility requires us to consider others and their needs more important than our own. Humility requires us to stand with the people, not over them; beside them, not above them. Humility requires a serving nature that withholds judgment and, instead, helps and comforts another because we are never certain about the sacrifices they have made to get where they are today. Humility, Topangah, tames our judgmental nature and motivates us to do more than our share to support, encourage, and meet the needs of others; it is a hard thing to grasp because it requires determination, courage, and a quiet dignity that gives us the freedom to serve another gladly as an outward expression of our love. Humility manifests itself in daily life. She who has it will gladly serve, often in awe of the unique and wonderful contributions people make while acknowledging and reinforcing their efforts. Humility invites unity, Topangah; it turns enemies into friends. Those who possess the deepest humility are those who possess the truest happiness, the greatest joy; humility is the vessel through which love pours among the people."

As a light wind swooped in spiraling currents, Sani paused. Topangah began to understand the harmony of the past has a way of healing the turmoil of the present. One is connected to the other by a power greater than humanity. It is for us to submit to that power, she thought; not to be enslaved but, rather, to be empowered by accepting all living beings are equal, an acceptance best expressed by putting others before ourselves.

"Before stepping into the river, Topangah, dip your hand into the water — earth's mirror — and touch it to your head. This is our way of giving thanks for the gifts the river brings, for the love that pours forth from her pebbled banks. This is our way of giving our respect to the river; to simply step in and take what we want does precious little to consider her needs before our own. Now step from the river's edge. Let the cold water run over your feet. Let her energy course through your body. It's the same energy that connects all of life. It makes us part of everything around us. Listen for the unspoken words and silences. The river, like Wolf, lives by voices we shall never hear. Their powerful and piercing songs carry on the wind and they, like us, are caught in a net between space and time that makes us sojourners, powerful and mysterious beings endeavoring to stay in balance with the world we share. Turn to the East, to the direction of Wolf, a place for determination and hope where all life begins, and close your eyes. Let the strength and radiance of the rising sun humble you with the refreshing awareness something much larger and much stronger than humanity serves us. Come to understand Grandfather Sun shines not on any one man or any one race of people alone; he shines on all. The seasons come and go for each of us. Love and friendship finds its way to all. As you think upon these things, Topangah, look to Wolf. Wolf, man's brother, bows its head in the presence of another, not because it has to but, rather, because it considers others before itself. Did you know it will not take food until that food can be shared with the pack? This enormous sense of family and this unfailing devotion to the pack demonstrates Wolf's respect for community and his willingness to humbly accept and submit without resistance to the will and desires of those around him. His is a quality of heart ready to submit himself to achieve what is good for others. He recognizes his place in the pack is no more important, nor more able, than another."

"Sani, I think what you are trying to tell me is that community is important to Wolf. Everything he does, it seems, is done for the greater good of the pack. He clearly has a great passion for living and much appreciation not only for the life he lives, but also for the pack he shares that life with. Though he may trot ahead, even out of sight, he always returns. Wolf is brave, patient, kind, and wise. Most of all, he is generous. There's much we can learn from Wolf, isn't there, Sani?"

"Yes, Topangah. Wolf is a great teacher. So good, in fact, he reminds us we are all teachers and students alike if we respect others and respect nature. Because Wolf lives in balance with nature rather than dominate over it, he need not posture; he understands — and accepts — the small part of the whole he plays as a deeply emotional, generous, genuinely affectionate, and quite gentle being. His fire and water — that is to say, his passion and compassion — are among his greatest gifts. Because Wolf understands all one needs is love, he is fully capable of providing it. He appreciates his insignificance. Yet, do not mistake what I say, Topangah. Wolf knows his place. He is large and beautiful. He is a magnificent being. His soul-piercing eyes penetrate us deeply. His presence is noble and powerful, yet not domineering. Wolf teaches us to possess a strong compassion capable of translating the love and gentleness we have for ourselves into the work and service we extend to others. Wolf's medicine helps us connect to that quiet place inside so we might gain our objectives through collaborative endeavors; he helps us connect to one another. He helps us realize we are one another. His message is the power to teach and share information. Where Wolf no longer roams, he is missed by every living thing in nature. Learn this kind of humility, Topangah. Push ahead on your own to become humble."

Topangah takes some time to think deeply about her relationship with Wolf. Before she can ask any questions, Sani speaks up. "Topangah, sometimes it's just you, the rain, and the wind. As a leader, a spiritual healer, a teacher, and a singer, it is up to you to be ever mindful of the people and their needs. You must endeavor to let understanding emerge through your words and actions so the people come to know how to balance light and shadow. Both are necessary to mark important passages of time. Though we, as a people, have undergone change for thousands of years, we are always in the now. How do we divide the old and the new? There is no beginning, no end, yet all we do becomes a marker, a story shared with many others that creates sacred space. You must always remember it is never easy, even for those among you who are strong, to be in a place where their vision is cut off, where the things they hear cannot always be seen. In such a world as ours, it becomes important for us to recall what can no longer be learned, and to see the past fully present. What has been forgotten, Topangah, is never truly lost; yet, it is not for you to bring a vision to the *Diné* but, rather, it is for you to uncover the people's vision and help bring it to life.

"Sani?"

"Yes, Topangah."

"I am not afraid of what is out there. I am eager to see it. This is my calling, it is what I want to do, but from where will come the message for how I should live my life?"

"Topangah, the message is all around you. Listen to your medicine. It helps you see what others cannot see. Spirituality, for us, is inseparable from all other aspects of our lives. Listen to the wind, to the sound of the river running through the narrow canyons below. Hear the bees, the rustling leaves, and the crackling fire. Seek the voices in your head, leaving the words behind. Then return to a place where there are no words; your heart knows your feelings, and your place in the world. Remember, silence leads to wisdom. You need only to listen. Your way of life has always been, and you are certain to find it."

"Can you help me learn how, Sani?"

"Yes, Topangah. I will help you. But you already know how. Tell *their* story, Topangah. Tell their story. You see, our stories — our collective voices — come from our common humanity. They are brought to us in the form of the Moonways, the Storyways, the Windways, the Rainways, the Lightningways, the Fire Danceways, and the Eagleways. We must care for the stories that come to us, and learn to give them away where they are needed, because it is through our stories we come to understand. Stories are how we care for one another."

"How so, Sani?"

"Topangah, storytelling transforms lives. Stories abound; their impact is typically wide and unconstrained. We rely on them every day in every facet of life. Story-telling has been around for as long as man has been around; it is as old as humanity itself. Remember the stories of The-Time-That-Was-Before; there you will find the good courage to look ahead to The-Time-That-Is-To-Be and come home to tell me about it. You see, Topangah, every tribe exists, in part, because of the stories others needed to tell. Storytelling is a gateway that opens our minds to new horizons, to the realm of possibility held against its will deep within the dominion of the impossible. Storytelling is powerful. It invites those who hear to widen an intimate awareness; storytelling nourishes the soul and expands the imagination. The stories we tell often exist across many dimensions to honor life; their meaning extends from the toils of everyday living to the extravagance of the divine. They embrace power befitting great chiefs, power that transcends time, matter, and space to groom connection and build relationships."

"Is this only true for our people, Sani?"

"No, Topangah. Though our heritage can divide us, the future awaits those who face their past. Consider the power of stories shared by others who toil in our midst — the Piaute, the Zuni, the Apache, the Havasupai, the Yavapai, the Pima, the Maricopa, the Papago, the Tewa, and the Hopi. Many are red, but others are yellow, white, and black. Across many cultures, this power draws from the strength of a circle. Our Lakotah brothers to the north who live in a land of flowing grasses and great plains teach us, 'In the circle, we are all equal. When in the circle, no one is in front of you. No one is behind you. No one is above you. No one is below you. The circle creates unity.'"

"I did not know there was such power in storytelling, Sani."

Just at that moment, the thunder cracked and exploded with an awesome power; lightning broke the sky in two as its radiance reached out in all directions. Soon a heavy rain began to fall. Both sat intently for a short time before Sani whispered to Topangah, "Do not forget. The power of words, like the sound of thunder, is not in the words themselves."

"Sani, it's just like my friend, Eagle."

"How so, Topangah?, Sani asked."

Taking a few minutes to contemplate Sani's question as the rain fell, she wisely points out, "Eagle works with the wind, Sani; he does not fight it. Nor does he tell the wind where and when to blow. Instead, he rides the wind, and goes where it takes him. It's as though the wind gives him the ability to live within the realm of the spirit world, yet remain connected and balanced with us in Earth Mother's realm."

Well pleased with Topangah's observation, Sani adds, "Eagle talks with you in your fasting and in your dreams. As he does, a great spirit keeps you company, giving *you* the ability to see beyond what you already know or have experienced. Stop, Topangah. Listen to him. Listen with your heart. Let your spirit soar with his. Then, and only then, speak. Speak the truth without demanding anything of another. This will set you free and give you the courage to help others find their own truth. Remember, Topangah, the world is big enough for all truth."

"Sani, how will I come to know this truth?"

"Look with me into the fire, Topangah. What do you see?"

"I see embers the color-of-the-setting-sun and small flames flickering first with the color-of-the-sky and then bright-as-a-flower. I see what remains of sweet smelling piñon limbs, cedar boughs, and small sticks and limbs from oak, juniper, white pine, and spruce. I see stones that keep their form, though they glow as bright as the stars above. In the fire's twilight, I see the yucca, cactus, sage brush, gramma grass, and wild flowers content to graciously yield their beauty all year round. Why, Sani?"

"Look again, Topangah. Look more closely, and *see* truth."

"Truth, Sani? How? Where?"

"Look for the deepest purple in the flame, Topangah. Truth comes to us in this form. Such is humility, Topangah. Do you understand? It says to us, even when we do not understand, that we share a destiny. The *Diné* look to us as their leaders for healing, and for teaching. They look for leading that serves, leading that gives and shares and cares. Like the piñon limbs and cedar boughs in our fire, we are expected to give of ourselves totally, to burn with the fiery trials of life that confront us and our community until we are reduced to nothing. We begin and end nowhere. We are everything, yet we are nothing. Unless we can truly find ourselves standing in the center, we are of little value. It is in this discovery of our humanity the humble soon forget themselves, Topangah, and they keep the fires lit until they, themselves, become as the purple flame, a purple flame that neither sets itself apart from others or above others, not to be over another, but to be *with* each other. Like a star's light reaching out in the deep of night from Father Sky, the light of the humble enters the hearts of her people and guides their way, a way in search of truth."

With that, Topangah looked deeply into the flame, deeper than ever before. There it was. Truth. Little did she know it had always been with her. Sani was right. Deep in the fire, like deep within her heart, truth illuminated the way of life, and now she had found it. Humbled by the discovery, she wanted to learn more. She was ever grateful.

"O' Great Spirit, thank you for guiding us here. Thank you for the care you have given us all this way. We will remember your kindness wherever we go. Thank you for all things and everything. Thank you for Mother Earth, Moon Woman, Father Sky, and Grandfather Sun. Thank you for the four directions: the east, the south, the west, and the north. Thank you for all my relations: the winged, the creeping, the crawling, the four-legged, the green and growing, and all things living in the water. Thank you for our Elder Brother, for Eagle, for Bear, for Buffalo, and for Wolf. Thank you for the light, the fields and orchards, the rivers and springs, health, homes, flora and fauna, animals, pebbles and stones, and love."

"O' Great Spirit, help us to learn how to live, how to find a path of beauty in this life that puts others before ourselves, and to know who we are with this beginning that we may understand our way is not to isolate good or bad from the rest of life, but to heal that which is sick and transform that which poisons us. Help us that we may come to know the deeper meaning of our song, a song that carries our prayers, a song that unites heaven and earth, spirit and matter, a song that brings us to the center of our being."

"O' Great Spirit, thank you that no matter where we find ourselves, we stand at the center of the universe, a place everywhere present at all times."

"O' Great Spirit, thank you for the purple fires that burn their way into the hearts of the *Diné*. Hear me, not for myself, but for everyone who is to come, and guide us to a new humility, a new understanding, a new purity, a new sincerity, and a new sense of truth."

6
Truth: Look to the Turtle for Understanding ~ It's the Journey that Matters!

My friends, … it does not require many words to speak the truth. What I have to say will come from my heart, and I will speak with a straight tongue.
~Hinmaton Yalatkit ((Chief Joseph)
aka, Thunder Rolling Down the Mountain)
Chief of the Wal-lam-wat-kain (Wallowa), Nez Percé

Sani was not in sight, yet Topangah knew where to find him. Of course, there was no rush. These last several days with Sani had changed Topangah's life — and the life of the people she would now serve — forever.

As the Morning Star rose prominently in the eastern sky, Topangah reflected upon her days on the mesa with Sani, ever grateful for each moment they share and for every lesson they learn together. The morning air was fresh and clean as Grandfather Sun directed his golden light with purpose across the desert, over the sandstone cliffs, along side the sandy washes, and against the scarred arroyos, searching out the purple shadows that seem to bring forth the best colors of Topangah's homeland — pinks and reds, magentas and browns, buffs and grays, yellows and greens — each exuberant among wind-twisted junipers and ancient piñons that stand determined against fear and indefatigable among the jagged rocks, secure in their strength and silence, persuasive in their fire and peace.

"Sani would appreciate this moment," Topangah thought to herself knowing just how much she would appreciate sharing it with him. So much so, it's as though she could hear his voice just now, carried by the wind, reminding her, "We must learn all we can from what is around us — the heavens, the birds, the changing seasons, the plants and animals, the rivers and streams, the land, the winds, the trees, the pebbles and stones, the mountains and sky — if we are to learn about that which resides within us."

The morning was still very young as Topangah quietly beheld the beauty of a new day, a day met with exuberance in the high-pitched, happy cries of her friend, Eagle. E-e-e-ya! E-e-e-ya! Watching him cross the sacred mountain's sloping curve and rise higher and higher above the magnificent mesa into the vast, cobalt dome of Father Sky, Topangah's fascination — and respect — steadily grew stronger as Eagle spiraled up, alternatively soaring and gliding with wings fully extended in an elegant dance of flawless beauty and grace. Like the spirit that always finds a pathway, Eagle's dance with Brother Wind follows the trail sweeping through the earth and sky that leads to unity, freedom, eternity, balance, and harmony, a well-worn trail stepping itself across the bluest of blue skies somewhere just below Grandfather Sun yet far above pillowed clouds that ripple like ocean swells to embrace Mother Earth with a perfect stillness, and a perfect peace.

Topangah turned and began walking to the east, knowing she would soon see Sani sitting cross-legged deep in meditation. Before him laid the great expanse of the valley trimmed, as it were, with the jutting indigo buttes that edged it. There was a timelessness on the old man's face, a look of great age sharply contrasted by a folded red scarf that bound his silver hair. His weathered dark skin, adorned with traditional clothing that hung loosely about his small, bony frame, displayed a meekness in his handsome aura as he sat with his wrinkled hands folded peacefully before him. As she turned to walk away, Topangah heard him softly whisper, "*Yah'ah' teh' ah'bin'eh.*"

"Good morning, Sani!," she excitedly replied. "Did you see Eagle!?"

"Yes, Topangah," Sani softly whispered. "Did *you* notice, as he soared free and unhampered like the wandering wind, how he wanted us to see him?," Sani asked.

"I did notice, Sani. Why do you think he wanted us to see him?"

"It would seem he has another very important lesson for us to learn, Topangah. As we've observed, Eagle takes his heritage where'er he goes; he forgets not who he is. His determined example demonstrates for *us* how to strive, how to overcome barriers, and how to lift opportunities among mankind. Eagle carries an absolute love in his heart that rekindles within the human spirit the desire to be better people, to embrace our role as caretakers of all life, to be friendly, to remember one another, and to keep an eye out for one another — not just fellow humans, but every living thing. He listens, and he teaches us to be still, for in our stillness Eagle knows we shall find the final harmony: silence. As we watch Eagle, we begin to *know* what it means to walk the Beauty Way, to be in balance. He reminds us our great power — knowing who we are — is best used to do good, to tell our stories, to dance, and to sing. Eagle is brave enough to live the way his heart tells him is right. As we, like Eagle, make our stand for love, Topangah, the people will come to know they always can find a way to keep harmony within their heritage, and to keep their heritage within their heart. Only then will they, too, be able to take their heritage where'er *they* go."

Sani's understanding of Eagle and his many valuable lessons of life, love and, for that matter, leadership, brings Topangah great delight. For her, there is no turning back even if, for a while, she must become skilled at living in two worlds. She knows Sani will help her learn those same valuable lessons and, for now, that's all that matters. Topangah knows Sani's words, on balance, are powerful. And she understands why. Yet, learning from him can be an intense, consuming experience for a young girl of twelve winters. There is no getting away from the dignified and stately meekness about his manner that, like Eagle, imbues those who are near with an ancient power to reflect, the strength of common spirit needed to heal, and a deep, abiding interest in the natural world. Those who follow in his steps along the Beauty Way share a resolute compassion for all things that enjoy life, an unfettered feeling of oneness, and a sacred spirit rising. As these thoughts go through her mind — and heart — Topangah thinks to herself, "I am never alone. Sani's words pursue — no, lead — me on my solemn walks along inner slopes of the canyon walls as I meander in and out of aged cliff hollows, up and down storied ravines, and to and from hallowed rock shelters, first curving back to the north before wrapping around to the south and east, carefree yet somehow expectantly surprised, as life's trail steadily winds westward before it abruptly descends like metered voice down switchbacks in anticipation of the valley floor only to make its way, once again, to the majestic glory of the mesa top. Along the way, Grandfather Sun's warm amber light, like Sani's words, find it easy to fill me with peace, trust, and goodness as the spirit of the breeze blows away my steps in the dust. Steps, like those of all who have walked this way before, that find the inner strength to shed any distrustful tenor of their ego before they are soon dispatched with the wind to walk wisely with Father Sky. Yet, as I think upon Sani's words, I find the encouragement to fear not what lies ahead on my path but, rather, to seize upon my unrelenting determination to stay on the path, the path of what I *know*, come what may."

Topangah's way of knowing sets her apart; it is strong, largely because it is her way to listen, especially to Sani. His countenance is as warm as sunlight, always shining bright among the *Diné*. He passes on stories — wonderful stories, filled with a sense of passion, presence, purpose, and place — handed down through the generations. His is the wisdom of a thousand years, and his words, like red embers of a warm and welcoming fire, burn and smoke with inspired sensibilities. Sani understands — and Topangah is quickly catching on — the *Diné* live by visions. They live by dreams. And they live by the subtle dignity of timeless truths.

"Sani?"

"Yes, Topangah."

"As my eyes watch what you do and my ears hear what you have to say, my heart learns your words are not only for me, but others besides. They matter to our people. They matter to people of every color. And they matter to every other two-, four-, six-, and eight-legged brother and sister just as much as they matter to the flying ones, to the crawling ones, and to those that slither among the grasses. They matter to those that swim in waters deep, and to the rooted ones that rise, like tall standing brothers. Your words pierce our hearts with truths to teach us all are one; past, present, and the future. You teach us life, whatever form it takes, is our brother and we cannot be separated from it. Like a song of laughter lifted upon the wind, your words teach us life brings an uncommon joy for those who can *see*. Your message is one of hope; it helps us to stop looking so we may see, and it reminds us the stones live, the rivers cry, the mountains breathe, the plants and animals hunger and thirst, and humanity yearns for beauty, a complete freedom found only in the spiritual *oneness* of creation where we experience the singularity of peace, in all of its might and strength, and in the stillness of the quiet reaches of our hearts and minds. Only in beauty can we spread our wings, like the wings of Eagle, to the fullest breadth of life. Sani, you — and, of course, Eagle — have taught me we are one family, united with an instinctive potential for compromise, tolerance, cooperation, and compassion. You are sacred, I am sacred, and the people are sacred. Together, *we* are sacred. From you, I have learned the world is good, and that same goodness reflects the sacredness in us all. Your life teaches in the absence of sacred, nothing is sacred."

"As you have observed, Topangah, it is our unity that makes us sacred. Spiritual oneness is the one great truth among all truths. That's why it is important for us, like Eagle, to love the goodness we share so we can put that goodness back into our world. Eagle need not dance alone with the wind. We, too, can dance with Eagle because our spirit soars with Eagle. We can dance with Eagle because we honor our visions and our dreams and, through them, we discern truth, and we gain all knowledge. We live as we have learned so we might fulfill our purpose in life and satisfy our yearning. Only when we remain true to ourselves can we understand — and speak — the whole truth. This is how we come to live lovingly, respectfully, courageously, honestly, humbly, and truthfully. Within the chiseled edges of a life so lived come the great gifts of wisdom and understanding and, through them, the hope of peace found only in our collective oneness."

"Sani, will there come a day when I am like Eagle?"

"You already *are* like Eagle, Topangah. Truth stands before you extending its great gifts, always at the ready to guide your steps. I see how you, like Eagle, look upon the great expanse of life, and all that goes on within it, as one who understands our connection, deeply and thoroughly. You already see that in life one must include, not exclude, and one must embrace, not deny. You understand what happens to one — stars, oceans, trees and plants, fields and orchards, springs, rivers and streams, woodlands, creatures and birds, humans, pebbles and stones, and other living things on Mother Earth — happens to all. You look upon life as one humble enough to *see* we are related, *mitakuye o'yasin*. Like Eagle, Topangah, you have willingly — and naturally — taken on a sacred responsibility to serve, to do your part to insure a good life, good air, and good water for all. You see the importance of every thing, that each thing matters. You understand even the tiniest star, as we look unto the heavens at night-middle-made, has a worthy place in the vast expanse of our world."

"Sani, tell me more about this word, *truth*. It is a word I think I do not understand."

Pausing to reflect, Sani recalls similar discussions during his visits with neighboring Taos Pueblo Elders. "Topangah, our brothers and sisters among the Taos Pueblo people tell me truth is a bright star dropped from the heart of eternity. *You* are that bright star, Topangah. And I am another."

"I am reminded, Sani, of the beauty in the designs on the potsherds of the great many kiva jars, bowls, and pieces of pottery the wind reveals as the ever-shifting desert sand moves across the baked clay children of 'the old ones' left behind to declare their handiwork and to tell their story. Is this *their* truth?"

"Topangah, truth is not found in the world, not even in the bold and vibrant designs of black on white pottery carefully coiled, scraped, smoothed, slipped, burnished, banded, painted, and fired a long time before, among the Anasazi; it is found within. Truth simply *is*. And it is most evident when we free ourselves to be ourselves."

"Just like the black on white pottery, Sani, where each pot wears its own distinctive beauty, but no two pieces ever are exactly the same."

"You speak wisely, Topangah. Who you are is truth. And who I am is truth. Those who look up to us and have chosen us to lead, heal, and teach them are truth. Who we are together is truth. What we are together is truth. What we are is beautiful! Beauty, looking upon all that lives with reverence and great love, is truth. Beauty is the discovery of balance and harmony in life; it is the essence of love. As we observe the rhythms of these ancient virtues, balance and harmony, we come to know how they, like truth, are at home among the *Diné*, yes, but also at home among the mesas, the buttes, the evergreen, the herbs, the grasses, the pollen, the morning mists, the dewdrops, the waters, the streambeds, the clouds, the winds, and all other forms of life, binding us one to another with a common spirit that fills our days with the joy of birdsong, fills our nights with a heavenly radiance, brings comfort to fellow creatures, great and small, and inspires unity where'er life's shadow dwells. To find the days and nights filled with song and a heavenly radiance is to find them filled with truth."

"When our days and nights are filled with truth, Sani, will our dreams draw closer, will our words speak more kindly to the people we meet?"

"Truth empowers us in many ways, Topangah. It possesses an enabling force to help each of us, as spiritual teachers, healers, singers, and leaders, go beyond the dreams of our hearts and go beyond the words we share to extend beautiful thoughts out across the earth and sky, thoughts belonging to *all* people, near and far, both those we have met and those we shall never know."

"What more must I learn about truth, Sani? Where do I begin?"

"Topangah, it is not a question of beginning. You now stand before the *Diné* as their spiritual teacher, healer, singer, and leader, and you *began* before you became conscious of the need to do so. What matters is becoming. Can you find the beginning of a circle, or the end? Does love have a beginning, or an end? Only where there is no beginning and no end can you find balance and harmony. Some call it beauty; others call it love, or truth. The circle of life is our best teacher. For us, life has no beginning and there is surely no end; only a change of worlds. To speak of life is to speak of you and me and love, these three. Such is the starting point of truth."

"What do you mean, Sani?"

Unknowingly, a long period of silence draws Topangah deeper into the beauty of Sani's lesson.

Topangah, thinking Sani may not have heard her question, was about to ask again when Sani said, "Moon Woman keeps watch by night. She is in perfect balance with Grandfather Sun who rises from the East at daybreak to wake Mother Earth and the people who call her home. Yet, we need not look further east of Grandfather Sun to a place of enlightenment and knowledge, nor further west of Moon Woman to a place of gratitude, or to the ends of Mother Earth to find truth. It always stands before us, with courage and purity of spirit, on its own two feet."

As Topangah caught herself scanning the mesa for any sign that truth was standing nearby, Sani picked up where he left off, reminding her, "Truth carries like deep thunder, yet it whispers like a soft breeze. It has no beginning and it never ends; it is as a circle that comes again unto itself. Truth permeates life and all that lives. It comes in every color, shape, and size. It can be found under a fallen leaf and it can be found high upon the tallest mountain. It can be seen with clarity in the darkest night and found with ease among the brightest stars. Its strength rests in its gentleness. It is majestic, yet meek. It is broad, yet to the point. Truth touches everything. Mostly, Topangah, it lets us be in touch one with another as, together, we come to share a love that passes understanding, a love that connects our hearts so we may learn how to walk with a greater knowledge and awareness of life, to walk with a greater sensitivity to others, to walk in beauty, the way of the *Diné*. It is the exchange of love that brings about a sacred trust, Topangah."

The wind blew softly against Topangah's face as she looked out over the mesa's rim beyond the dark blue buttes to the great, uncluttered distance that seemed to mark the farthest reaches of her beloved homeland among the pink sand, the desert winds, and the golden sunsets that gave definition — and high relief — to the majestic mesas. In her contemplation, her piercing brown eyes betrayed the wonder and the majesty of where she was, and how she got here. Only moments passed before Sani added, "Consider Grandmother Turtle."

"The turtle, Sani?"

"Yes, Topangah. We look to Grandmother Turtle to help us understand truth. Both are strong, self-reliant, and resolute; theirs is a quiet communication with the thunder that speaks intuitively to the heart. Both are slow and deliberate. Both are patient. Both are strong and stable. Both teach us all created things depend on our love and understanding, just as we depend on them. Even as Turtle cannot separate herself from her shell, truth cannot stand outside itself, nor can *we* separate ourselves from our connection to all living things. Without the others, Topangah, we would soon come to know we are lost. Yet, we need not fear; we are bound by love. And we are bound by truth. Truth reveals itself to love. Like Grandmother Turtle, truth teaches us it's the journey, not the destination, that matters."

"Isn't that what the heart teaches, too, Sani?"

"What we have been taught, Topangah, is that she alone sees who sees with her heart. Your heart remembers the truth even if your mind forgets. It's *see*-ing, not saying, that brings us closer to truth. I have heard it said many times among our people, 'it does not require many words to *speak* truth.' Knowing truth is very important if we are to act wisely and prevent harm. Truth shows itself in the total silence that comes, like a summer's rain, after we have freed our self of another's judgment. Truth resides deep in the moment among the quiet recesses of our heart. We can be certain our past informs our present and influences our future, yet our *Satsika*, or Blackfoot, brothers teach us to dwell not on the past nor contemplate the future; to do so loses sight of the moment, the only real truth. In this truth, as in the old, sacred Turtle, we find all that we need. Truth lies in spirit and, though it may be slow in coming, the time for truth is now; it is omnipresent. It is always there."

Topangah liked the idea of truth all around her, and all around the *Diné*. It was both comforting, and fulfilling. Maybe it was because the wisdom of the Elders, seeking as they may to blend the real with the unreal and the true with the false, brought her within reach of her own very personal understanding of truth, and closer to wisdom's great motivator: love. For this insight, Topangah was especially grateful.

"O' Great Spirit, thank you for the good red road, the spirit road that leads to the Beauty Way, where there is only love, and truth that connects our hearts as one."

"O' Great Spirit, thank you for Grandmother Turtle, and for her patience and persistence. Help me to be more like her, to always speak the truth quietly, but only after I have listened with an open mind and a servant's heart. Help me to remember the peace that is found only in the stillness of the final harmony, silence."

"O' Great Spirit, thank you for the teachings of the wind that help us come to know the value of presence. Thank you for Mother Earth and the way she makes for us through this life, for the food that sustains us and keeps us breathing, and for the water we drink when our body is dry. Thank you for a gracious Grandfather Sun who warms us throughout our lives. Thank you for a caring Moon Woman who, through the night, watches over each of us as equals, one related to another. Thank you for fire that purges our path of the obstacles that hinder our journey. Thank you for teaching us to love."

7
Wisdom: Live as the Busy Beaver ~ Uncover Your Gifts and Use Them to Build Big Dreams, Do Some Good, and Make a Difference!

The manner with which we walk through life is each man's most important responsibility, and we should remember this with every new sunrise.
~Thomas 'Medicine Rock Chief' Yellowtail,
Crow Medicine Man and Sun Dance Chief

Everything around Topangah felt new and wonderful as she and Sani prepared for their journey home. Taking special notice of the pink sands accenting the tan and brown patchwork swatches of desert earth prostrate at the feet of deep red canyon cliff faces delicately carved in sandstone walls by gentle wind spirits, Sani quietly came to terms with limitations of his own. He would soon complete his work, having done all he could to serve the needs of his people and, more recently, prepare Topangah for the path that now lays before her to follow. Topangah, he reasoned, walks the Beauty Way, just as Sani has walked it, with deep respect and admiration for Creation; in good kinship, she walks in harmony, balance, abundance, and peace among her relations who, like her, seek the comfort of the four sacred mountains that hold up the *Dinetah*, mountains that allover and at once connect Topangah to her forever home, mountains certain to nourish and sustain her without end. For now, Sani believed it was enough to know the shadows of this place grow long, joining with light and shade to magnify the mesa's majestic array of color into a seamless tapestry teeming with the beauty of many familiar forms. But Sani, it seems, is not the only one taking notice of the shadows' steady march. Perhaps it was the glorious melding of color or, more simply, the softened light that comes with the passing day. Whatever it was, Topangah found herself happy and deeply contented to be in the presence of a magnificent man who had lived many moons, so many she supposed, that no one of her tribe, not even the Elders, can likely recall a time when Sani wasn't old. This thought comforted her like no other, making it easy for her to ask, "Sani, how did you get to be so wise?"

Sani, naturally, was struck by the sudden directness of the question. Certainly, he expected it at some point, just not now. Not while the two of them marveled at the beauty beaming from the shadows. "The secrets of life," he thought to himself, "are found in the deepest crannies of shadow. It is what one leaves behind. And it is the first place to look if we are to *see* what needs must be seen. Truth," Sani observed, "resides among the light and shadow, somewhere between the white and black, where opposites are often as shiny as chipped pebbles smoothed, rounded, and polished by river's timeless touch." In the fleeting moments, Sani's thinking escaped the silent citadel of his mind and sweetly rang out, piercing the silence of the open mesa as he voiced what could only be spoken from deep within his heart: "They always deserve the truth."

"Who deserves the truth?," Topangah asked thoughtfully, leaving her previous question for another time.

"Sometimes great thoughts stir the consciousness, Topangah, and lift from our lips like the fragile pink petals of peach blossoms rising on a gentle summer's wind. Often, without our consent," Sani added with a warm, familiar smile before continuing. "Wisdom is like that, I believe. It commonly comes to the people in many forms. I am no different in that regard. Experience truly is our best teacher. We do things, and we learn from them. We live and life teaches us. With a profound courage, we seize the strength to let go, to try new things, to strive, to move on ... and to fail, even as we *know*-ingly seek out new experiences, some easy to remember while others are not so easy to remember. You see, Topangah, it's in our remembering we come to know."

"Know what, Sani?," Topangah eagerly asks.

"The Old Ones, the Elders, do not devote their lives to preserving the wisdom of their fathers and their grandfathers; instead, they experience it. They 'walk' the ancient ways and they live out the sacred knowledge passed down from age to age. This is how they give spiritual direction to the *Diné*. The people watch, and they, too, remember as the wisdom, courage, and strength of a thousand years flow through the Old Ones, and through me. For this reason, Topangah, you will soon come to *know* what my grandfather knew and what his grandfather before him knew. You will know what the mothers and the grandmothers know. Look first to the East — all things begin in the East. Now look to the West, and understand. The East, Topangah, brings new beginnings while the power we find in the West brings change marking an end to our day. In the East we find our making; our unmaking is found in the West. Yet both our making and our unmaking help us keep our balance. They bring harmony into our life. When we are still — where the silence joins us to balance and harmony — we learn there is a wind that tumbles, Topangah, and only when we stand against this wind can we create the kind of change no other force can bring. Harness this wind, Topangah. Be its friend. Grow strong by its side, because the journey from East to West, no matter how many moons one must trek, compares precious little to the journey you, and you alone, must make in another dimension, the certain but uncompromising journey that lies between your head and your heart."

"How so, Sani?"

"There exists a blindness, Topangah, some say of ignorance while others more hopeless than the first say of contempt, that lingers in the darkness unsure if the East shall ever find its way to the West, yet a light, the light of wisdom, shines in our midst; it never perishes. Not unlike the deep, bright blue sky always present above dark stormy clouds, wisdom may disappear, largely hidden behind a veil of misunderstanding, but it is always within our reach, always at the ready to liberate the *Diné* from self-imposed limitations and the short-sighted expectations of others. Wisdom, like a bright light, lifts humanity; illuminating the present moment, it empowers, and heals, the people. This is important, Topangah, because the present moment holds no beginning and no end. The same must be said of our journey. Until we realize our life's work, our journey, is not about the destination, there's no where to go. All we require to fulfill the old we can find in the new. It is how we come to understand what others cannot know. All the answers lie right where you'd expect them," Sani says while pointing to her heart. "Within." Some moments pass before Sani continues, "Let me show you. Look up, and then look down. What do you see?"

"I see what you see, Sani. As Grandfather Sun smiles upon us in all of his glory from above and our grassland brothers trouble themselves to make our measured journey tolerable, if not more pleasant, here below, I see shadows dancing with the light."

"Topangah, we see shadows precisely because they move; their dance gives us something to believe in, something to hold on to, something to know. To watch the shadows is to watch us dance, and to watch us dance, our Hopi brothers and sisters are fond of saying, is to *hear* our hearts speak. Our knowing, Topangah, comes from *see*ing. If we are to see clearly, we must first learn to listen with our eyes. Close your eyes. Now tell me what you *see*."

"Listen with my eyes? To *see*?" After a brief time, Topangah remarks, "Sani, we *can* hear hearts speak! When we find ourselves in a sacred place, they teach us we, ourselves, become sacred. Only a few days ago I suggested your life teaches me nothing is sacred in the absence of the sacred. Now I know the sacred exists whether we *see* it or not. Even where there is shadow, there must be sacred. You've shown me sacredness 'is' ... or it 'isn't' ... there's no in-between. *We* are sacred just as sacred is us. If we see goodness in our world, we are blessed to also see sacred. If we are unable to see goodness in our world, we are still blessed to see sacred, even if we do not recognize it for what it is. When I listen with my eyes, I recognize the world is good, Sani, and that same goodness reflects the sacredness in us all. It must, because without sacred, there is no *us* and, without us, the world is less than it could be. We and sacred, Sani, are one."

"Yes, Topangah, but don't stop there. Again, tell me what you *see*."

"Like the many colors that surround us, what I see above and what I see below are not the same yet, somehow, they are exactly the same. They are deeply connected, just as you and I are connected. Perhaps, Sani, it is *because* you and I are connected. Our lives, it seems, converge to connect above with below or, maybe, above and below converge to connect our lives one to another, or both. What is easy to see is we cannot separate one from the other. Above, below, and our lives here in between are the same. Is there no in-between? To merely look with our eyes, it seems, is to miss all there is to see, and hear."

"I am pleased, Topangah. This day, you looked, just as you have looked every day before, and all things appeared differently. Yet, you can *see* they have not changed at all. You have. Don't be afraid to be different. As the things above and the things below become part of you, come to know yourself. To know others, look from your heart and you will hear all you need to see. In this knowing, where you learn to listen, you soon begin to accept all without judgment. You come to appreciate the other's view because you learn what it is like to walk their trail."

Perhaps for the first time, Topangah noticed how the lines in Sani's face show the many *trails* he has walked in his life. She then returned to a question she asked earlier, "Is this how you came to be so wise, Sani?"

"All I have learned, Topangah, can be summed up like this: be in awe of life, be at peace and, when possible, be of some assistance to another." After a long pause, Sani added, "There's one more thing."

"What is it?"

"Be love. You see, Topangah, the *Diné* matter because love matters. Love transcends humanity; it is the inescapable *truth* of life. More than that, love is the essence of all that lives; it is utterly and outright essential. Love is what we need it to be. It is the pebble in the stream, the mountaintop among the clouds, the grass that blows in the wind, the shadows dancing among the lights, Grandfather Sun and the Moon Woman, the people who walk by and those who stick around a while. Love is every living thing. You and I are love.

The *Diné* are love. When we want to see/be with love, we have only to look upon/stand with the hearts of those in our midst, not forgetting, of course, our own heart. Love is manifest in the work of our heart, Topangah, and our part in that work cannot be obscured, or overlooked. Not to put too fine a point on the matter, *we are* because love is. Love is the same everywhere, in all realms. It extends beyond mere emotion to connect one species to another in an intricate web that strengthens and fortifies life. It is why we heal, why we teach, why we sing, and why we lead our people. It is what makes us truly wise. Love, Topangah, is not something we take along for our journey; it *is* the journey."

Topangah thoroughly enjoyed listening to and learning from Sani. She hung on every word, every gesture, and every song, spoken and unspoken. As she drew deeply from the truth he shared, she heard him quietly say, "Look, as I do, to Beaver — *Chaa'* — for wisdom."

"Beaver, Sani?"

"Topangah, wisdom is discovered all along your journey through this life. In an eagle, our Lakotah brothers and sisters from the northern plains often say, there is all the wisdom of the world. Wisdom can also be found in the fragrant petals of a wild flower, in the strong winds that tear at your hair, in the face and words of an Elder, in the first rays of Grandfather Sun, and in the busy life of Beaver. As you listen, you will come to *see* it in every sound; as you look, you will come to *hear* it in every form. Wisdom is our unique gift. Each of us is created special; you are one of a kind, as am I. So, too, is each wild flower, strong wind, and golden ray. Watch, Topangah, and hear. Observe life in its many forms — the four-legged, winged, creeping and crawly ones, and those who dwell among the stars. All living spirits, and each small voice, sings in its own way. Together, a thousand voices tell a single story. They are telling your story. You are telling their story. Topangah, knowledge is learned; we hear it in our stories. Wisdom, however, must be lived. Live, and learn, Topangah."

"What can you tell me of Beaver, Sani?"

"As a master of water and wood, *Chaa'*, Beaver, teaches us to uncover and understand our gifts, and to use them well. Beaver is a friend to all that make their home in its territory, and it takes great care to look beyond its own needs. For Beaver, community is inclusive; it always reaches out to others. Beaver is creative, productive, and persistent. Strength and trust are counted among Beaver's best friends. Beaver has a strong sense of family, and it appreciates each other's limitations, gifts, and talents. Beaver possesses a gentle nature, but it favors action. It is not enough for Beaver to dream big dreams; it must bring those dreams to life. Beaver doesn't linger, nor does it obstruct opportunity. Success comes largely because Beaver decides for himself the work to do and how best to get it done."

Raising her eyebrow ever so slightly, Topangah asks, "What do you mean by that, Sani?"

"There's much worthwhile work for Beaver to do. If there was any question as to the value of this work, things would be left undone. Beaver's strength of character carries the day, but Beaver's physical strength carries the community. Beaver does the work that needs doing, and he does it not only for his own benefit, but for the benefit of all who live nearby. Beaver, through his many abilities and talents, shows us how to live in harmony with the world around us, even as that world consistently undergoes change. Above all, Beaver is tenacious and determined. His spirit is indefatigable. But he doesn't reach for the sky."

"What does that mean, Sani?"

"*Chaa'* is practical and resourceful, Topangah. He sets goals, realistic goals. These goals matter to the community at large. That's because many community needs are met with steady, consistent effort and some imagination. Beaver is happiest when working with others, and he realizes he is not the only one to dream. Others dream, and their dreams, not unlike his own, are respected and acted upon to build a better life for all. You see, Beaver has a kind and gentle spirit, encouraging us with a quiet and steady influence. We would all do well to be more like Beaver."

"Sani?"

"Yes, Topangah."

"Maybe it's just me, but it seems Beaver is more concerned about what *we* do well together than in knowing, somehow, what one may do not-so-well alone. Even if some may lack understanding, Sani, Beaver persists in his worthwhile work, eager to do well with dignity, compassion, and humility knowing there are many paths to what one truly loves. Truth, balance, and harmony find a refuge in his actions. Again and again, we can see Beaver gives of himself expecting nothing in return, content to contribute his gifts (such as insight, ingenuity, enthusiasm, and sharp teeth!) for the good of the world, and to further a peaceful, strong, and healthy community. I have learned from you, and Beaver, our spirits grow weak when we fail to understand the gifts we possess, and to use those gifts in a good way. When we fail to honor knowledge and apply its teaching to our lives, we become hindered, unable to thrive. That's why I think it is important for us to learn from *Chaa'* to cherish knowledge and, with time, come to know Wisdom as our friend and to use that kinship for the good of the *Diné.*"

"Topangah, your words are true. *Chaa'* teaches us to learn all we can about our surroundings and our world," Sani insists, "because there is a kindness, a silence, and a quiet gentleness inside our own heart and, as you have learned, our hearts speak to the dance we hear as the songs we see rise steadily from Mother Earth, carried by wind, fire, water, and spirit to the four directions. As we discover how to truly hear, we come to appreciate the songs — songs for dancing, singing, healing — because we learn every living thing has a song. We also come to know who we are. As the many songs of life grow louder, and as we come to better understand, the many songs become as one: we call it 'harmony' — the subtle, soft, but strong tolerance that grows from our unconditional love for another. These songs teach and, having learned new things and new songs, it is for us to return to our people and to share what we know so, together, we may change and grow, and better our lives through the knowledge of life. We learn to act on our dreams so we may bring them to life. This is the wisdom we learn from *Chaa'*, our Beaver friend."

Topangah listened intently to all Sani had to say. Often, she noticed, Sani talked with his eyes, kind and full of understanding, and full of love. Sani always made it clear to her love is never withheld from another, nor is it horded and kept for self. Love is for sharing, always. The gift of love helps others experience their worth, and it stimulates their potential by coming into one's heart only after self, what some call ego, is removed. Because true love is selfless, it is also expandable; it scales to encompass all life. As an outward manifestation of the Great Spirit, we can see what love does. It heals. It makes all things a little better than before. Clearly, there is much to learn, but there is no denying Topangah feels Sani's love, and she feels perfectly at ease asking any question knowing in her heart he always answers with gentleness, and only with gentleness. Love, she reasoned, does not see the differences among us; instead, it looks upon the many similarities we share. It binds us together to weave our destiny. So, too, does our friend on high.

E-e-e-ya! E-e-e-ya!

"Sani! Did you hear that!?"

E-e-e-ya! E-e-e-ya!

"I hear him again! Do you hear him?"

"I hear him, Topangah. He bids you farewell."

Topangah knew this to be true. Before Grandfather Sun puts the day away, she and Sani would be back with their family.

"How does he know we are leaving today, Sani?"

"Eagle, above all others Topangah, can see both sides of the mountain. Through him, you have come to know love more fully. And, like him, you now can rise above situations and be free. You have learned Eagle is a sign of power and love. And the wind beneath his wings lifts the power of your thoughts higher and higher, to fly deeply into the beauty beyond this world. Eagle gives you the freedom to follow your own trail, Topangah."

"I am grateful for his presence, Sani. He flies to the distant shores of my hopes and dreams. Always eager to remind me of love's light, he fills my world with beauty beyond what I can imagine. Our northern Lakotah friends speak the truth, Sani. In Eagle, there *is* all the wisdom of the world!"

"Topangah, there is all the wisdom of the world in *you*, too. Like Eagle, it's the love in you that the people love, and it's the beauty in you the people love. Through this love, this wisdom, your words fall softly into the quiet of our hearts as you sing of things the people have forgotten, things like dignity, peace, unity, acceptance, compassion, tolerance, humility, gratitude, truth, respect, and love. Your song tells of a love that knows no limits and has no bounds, always trusting, sharing, and giving. Topangah, your gift to the people, a chance to see things as they could be, is rare and will be well-received. As you teach us to let our love expect

and demand nothing, but fulfill everything, at least for a
moment, for another, we shall remember, and we shall be
forever grateful."

As she thought upon her new life, Sani restated what
both already knew: "In these last days, Topangah, you have
learned much, especially about yourself. This is but the
beginning. And it is a good beginning. You and the Old Ones
are now somehow alike; you share a common bond. It is up
to you to learn all you can from them; sadly, they are all that's
left who remember the old ways. The truths they speak must
never be forgotten. Because you already possess their soft-
spoken, gentle wisdom, these teachers will quietly come into
your life when you call them. Look for them, and watch as
they pass their wisdom from generation to generation. Hear
their voice. Remember the old ways found in ceremonies,
ancient traditions, sacred songs, dances, and teachings among
our people. Discover and embrace new things in the old.
Make room for your understanding, and nurture a growing
respect and honor for differences among those who live,
learn, and love within your midst. Be patient, knowing
understanding comes softly, and in its own time. While you
wait, share our knowledge. In time, Topangah, you will be my
age; along the way many more will see, hear, and remember.

This is how it should be. But it will not be easy. The *Diné*, a grateful people, must first enter a time of great change, even a time filled with chaos and destruction, a time of purification. They will ask you to lead them, to teach them, to heal them, and to sing their songs. From our stories, music, dance, art, sacred symbols, and ceremonies, never forget we have always come to know the love, joy, and peace of such times, times made beautiful through pure relationships and a profound awareness that brings us to a spiritual harmony and balance in our world."

This was as much as Topangah thought she could bear. But Sani knew better, and this was far too important to leave something undone. "Topangah," he gently spoke, "as you rise each morning, the people will look for you to give thanks for another day. Our people are bound to a time of preparation. There's a time to decide which road to take, a time to heal, a time to look within for goodness, and a time to look for the goodness within others. Mother Earth and Father Sky teach us what we need to know, and we have come to know one cannot flourish without another. We may have separate roles, but we are equal, one to another. So it is with all people."

"What are you saying, Sani?"

"In finding the strength and good courage to discover and embrace the things we share, we begin to respect and honor our differences. Understanding and forgiveness somehow make us more compassionate. As we learn how to live together in harmony, we begin to hear one another's cry, we make room for healing, and we find our balance. We accumulate wisdom."

Thinking about everything Sani had said, Topangah knew it was not enough to accumulate wisdom. There was more. Taking this opportunity to share her understanding, she said, "We remember. We share. And the circle begins again."

Sani smiled inside. He smiled on the outside, too, having noticed Topangah nervously fidgeting with something in her hands.

"What do you have there, Topangah?"

"Grandmother gave these to me before I left. The small deerskin squares contain tobacco and red willow bark. I am to burn them for sacrificial offerings when I have need."

"Grandmother has powerful medicine, Topangah."

"Yes, Sani. I know. She also has visions that she will help me to see when I return to her."

"I, too, will help you *see*, Topangah. I have tried my very best to recall all I have learned in life, and to share it with you. You're ready to go out on your own now. Use what I have taught you to help others. They will know you carry strong medicine. And they will know you are a singer. As you begin your walk, remember I am not a medicine man and you are not a medicine woman. Instead, we are caretakers of sacred knowledge. That's all we are. The medicine we carry is not the herbs, the chants, the pipes, or the songs we sing. Our medicine comes from our willingness to help others attain that which is good in life. We are to take our natural talents, which may not seem like much to you at the moment, and bring them together with our promise to use those talents to enrich, encourage, empower, and transform other lives, indeed all life. Each day we live gives us another opportunity to use our gifts, to build a peaceful world, and to lose ourselves, for the good of others, in a labor of love. It is the same for any true leader in any setting, Topangah."

They walk along in silence much of the day. The sky is blue, white with clouds, and the air is filled with birdsong.

The sound is so beautiful everything everywhere listens. It is the sound of truth. Just before entering the village, Sani encourages Topangah with one last word of advice.

"Topangah, you have been set on a different path. Do not be anxious. There is a reason. As the people look to you for spiritual direction, teachings, and healing, they also will look for you to share your song like you share your life and all that you possess. Every goodness, you will learn, must rise from your trail like the thin wisp of smoke that rises, as you can now see, from our homes. The people will live a better life knowing you will give them your heart. Bring cheer into their midst. Lift their spirits, even at most difficult times. Strengthen them and fill them with hope. They have good hearts, Topangah. Always remember the ancient teachings of our friends: nothing will happen until something good can be done about it. And do not fear what you do not know. Seek goodness, Topangah, and you shall surely find it. Embrace the people with a love so deep it manifests in simple forms we have come to value: respect, honesty, humility, patience, faith, and kindness. The people will see the wisdom rise from the warmth of your unselfish and compassionate ways. Because wisdom is the outcome of your giving, caring, and sharing, it will establish, and affirm, your place among the

Diné. Inspire them to stand their full stature as a people, to weave the pattern of their destiny with courage and pride, and to dare to see themselves for who they truly are. Now go, and take care of the people."

With that, Topangah pondered the many lessons, and the simplicity of all she had learned. The greatest lesson Sani taught her was that no story should go untouched. In her moment of reflection, she lifted her eyes toward Grandfather Sun and, with a heart filled with gratitude, offered her thanks:

"O' Great Spirit, thank you for the harmonious unity of all forms of life."

"O' Great Spirit, thank you for the mighty bear, the tiny mouse, the fast squirrel, the slow turtle. Thank you for the bright sun, the shady tree, the cool breeze, the still stone. Thank you for the tall corn, the round squash, the tiny bean, and thin roots. Thank you, Mother Earth, for giving me life."

"O' Great Spirit, thank you for Grandfather Sun's life-giving aid to all living and growing things. Thank you for helping me look beyond eagle-feather fans, that I may hear in the winds of silence that carry the sounds of distant drums what I long to see. Thank you for our language, thank you for our beadwork, thank you for my jingle dress, and thank you for the celebration of life."

"O' Great Spirit, whose voice I hear in the winds, lead me on the path of the heart. Thank you for helping me to see the answers to life's many important questions lie within; they belong to the realm of love. Thank you for helping me to see walking the path of the heart is a great honor. Thank you for helping me be fully accountable for myself."

"O' Great Spirit, thank you for wisdom. Help me to understand how to live. Help me to understand how to get by with what you have given me. Help me to treat other people like I want them to treat me. Help me see the beauty of life."

"O' Great Spirit, thank you for helping me see that beyond our different beliefs, cultures, colors, languages, and religions, we are very much the same; we are brother and sister, we are one."

8
The Singer ~ Where-Mountain-Meets-The-Sea

"The Elders say, 'The longest road you're going to have to walk is from here to here. From your head to your heart.' But they also say you can't speak to the people as a leader unless you've made the return journey. From the heart back to the head."
~Phil Lane, Yankton (Dakotah) and Chickasaw tribes
Founder of Four Worlds Development Project,
University of Lethbridge, Alberta, Canada

Everything a Navajo knows — the hogan, ceremonies, *Yádiłhił Shitaá* (Father Sky), horses and sheep, snakes and insects, *Shimá Nahasdzáán* (Mother Earth), and all that manifests the wonderment of creation — is holy. But nothing is more sacred, more loved, or more respected by the *Diné* than the beautiful, rugged land they call home. Their beloved *Dinetah* — at once, both a mystery and a love story — is a land of astonishing splendor set in the middle of flat, alluvial valleys stunningly framed in painted swathes of sweetgrass, sage brush, piñon groves, and juniper-clad sun-painted mountains standing tall behind towering redstone cliffs and fire-colored mesas.

As Grandfather Sun dances across the sky, one can feel the air of expectancy thicken and settle over the land; a sweet anticipation, keyed with a magical wonder, prevails. Centuries-old adobe dwellings, clearly visible, are among the first signs of home as Topangah's senses fill first with the smells of braided chamisa, rabbitbush, juniper, and white sage, then the sounds of ceremonial *hatals* (sings) carried across the mesa on welcoming winds.

"Sani, are you nervous?"

"No, Topangah. I am not nervous. Why do you ask?"

"I don't know. I guess I just want to make sure you are looking forward to our reception. You know, with all those people and all."

"What are you saying, Topangah? Are *you* nervous?"

"Nervous? Me? What reasons do I have to be nervous? Why, I am as calm as …, hmmm. Well, okay. I might be a little nervous."

"Why are you nervous, Topangah?"

"I don't know how I will be received by the people, Sani."

"You don't know how you'll be received by the people who love you? Surely you recall how they reacted to your departure? Do you have reason to believe your return should be any different?"

"I know my family misses me, Sani. But I wonder if their demands will be too great for me to endure, the burden of leadership too great to bear. What will they say? What are their expectations? Can I meet those expectations? What am I to do from here on out? Am I ready?"

"I suppose this is natural, Topangah, but totally unnecessary."

"What do you mean, Sani?"

"At this very moment, Topangah, your Navajo family is filled with great expectation. A fourth day of ceremony and prayer heralds your arrival; your stories have been long awaited. With measured anticipation, they are lighting braided bundles to bless your home with the smoke of sweet-smelling grasses and sage. Tonight, in the afterglow of sundown, there will be elaborate rituals and much dancing. Everything we shall see and experience affirms our place in the circle of life and brings to our hearts and minds all the meaning and all the beauty of Mother Earth. The dance will go on for hours beneath a climbing moon. When the great dance-potlatch is over, there will be food — beef (whole cows), red chili stew, green chili stew, chicken with rice broth, *posole* (pork and cabbage stew with a zesty touch of cilantro), fresh bread baked in the outdoor *horno*, fry bread, apples, peaches, and sweet bread pudding — and gifts and, of course, the welcome for our return."

"I'm still nervous, Sani."

"It is fear that grips you, Topangah. From an early age we are taught to fear, yet the wisdom we, as a people, seek comes only to those who have unlearned fear."

"How do we unlearn fear, Sani?"

"Ours is a world of illusion, Topangah. This illusion is most evident in our fear of belonging, our fear of falling short of another's expectations, our fear of failure, our fear of letting others down, and our fear of the unknown. Fear, largely a distorted reflection of our inner being, shrouds us within a thick, dark veil. Fear is never what we think it is; neither is time. In our rush to align ourselves with what we can see, we can become completely unaware of how we are already thoroughly connected with the whole, that we possess a unique oneness with all of our relations. Sadly, fear makes us unable to *see*. But there is hope. If we are to regain our sight, we need only to seize the power of the present moment. It alone provides the true reflection of the oneness with life we hold deep within. We call it love, Topangah. As you have already discovered, fear and love cannot coexist. As we learn to love, we unlearn fear. So you see, there is no reason to experience fear."

"Why not?"

"Because, Topangah. We possess within ourselves the truth of who we are, a knowing that we are somehow never alone, that our steps are guided, and that we go where we are sent. All things are part of the whole, the circle of Grandfather Sun, Moon Woman, Father Sky, Mother Earth, and the winds that surround us and keep us going, winds that bring strangers — and balance — our way to teach us the value of presence. Throughout our lives, being present is the best gift we can share with another; it is patently more powerful than anything we can otherwise say or do. As you have learned, we are not bound by past, present, or future. Time has no hold on you or me; it is circular, not linear. It is also singular. By that, I mean the only place of power, the only place to serve and to serve well, is the present moment. That's because we come to know the world — and our place within it — differently when we serve it. You see, Topangah, his grandmother and her grandfather are your grandmother and grandfather. We are one family. We share one world. We come together as one humanity. Besides, what would life be if we had no courage to attempt anything? Dance with Bear, Topangah, and remember it is for us to love, not to fear. Rather than blame the darkness, as is the custom of so many, let us, instead, stand with an uncommon courage to illuminate the way ahead, to *uncover* the darkness and free us from the grip of fear. As we find ourselves on the other side of fear, we find we are, indeed, never alone; kindness, peace, and love are there to keep us company."

"Love is there all the time, isn't it, Sani?"

"Yes, Topangah. Love really is all we need, because it is what the people so desperately seek. It is love that connects us, Topangah, if we but love all without constraint and without condition."

"You make it sound so simple, Sani. So, why do I get the feeling it will be difficult?"

"It is largely because you have not yet walked in the steps our Elders have left behind. An Elder's teacher is the fire. Undefined by age or gender, it is the Elder who walks with humility to carry the knowledge of our traditions in truth and dignity. We can often find them embracing the wisdom of the heart in their sweat lodges, along mountain streams, by our tall standing brothers, and before Grandfather Sun. No matter where we find them, they are never alone. The stones, corn, tobacco, water, and the seven grandfathers keep them company as, together, they graciously serve the people."

As Sani paused to further collect his thoughts, Topangah considered how the Elders embody our collection of stories; as storytellers, they live the lessons their stories teach. Topangah then took the time to reflect on all of the stories Sani must have told over the years, knowing each story gives life to the people and, as she did so, she began to feel the love and excitement of all the small children who, at one time or another, gathered around his aged lap on long, cold, winter nights. There is a gentleness and an inherent kindness about Sani, she reasoned, that quiets even the most troubled spirit. "Clearly, the way of the ancients is a very gentle way," she told herself.

"Think upon Eagle, Topangah. Flying higher than any other creature, he sees life just as he sees love; both are continuous with neither a beginning nor an end. For Eagle, nowhere is everywhere, and everything is nothing. Time loses its contours. We soon learn the present is the only *time* that matters because it conceals the power of profound awareness. In the present we share the same story, a story we are able to see only through awareness. That doesn't mean we are here to live out another's story. We are, however, supposed to learn from them as we live out our own story. It is true my story is another's story, and their story is my story; indeed, everything we need is in the story of another. Truth, inseparable from who you are, is only as far away as the next story. Fragments, woven together, complete our story, and make us whole. That's because *you* are the truth. In our weaving comes authentic expression; as we are empowered to write, sing, dance, paint, and share our story, we help another find what they are looking for ... right where it's always been. Within. From many, Topangah, comes one voice. In that voice — captivating, mesmerizing, and richly reverberating with deep truth — community is born. So, too, is our courage to love, and lead, with no fear."

"I love long winter days when the Elders sit around telling stories about the-time-that-was-before. Sani, I was wondering."

"About what, Topangah?"

"Well, I was wondering if every community has a story?"

"Communities, and the stories they tell, Topangah, strengthen and reinforce the character of the people; through social bonds, they are thought to embrace shared values and empower moral voice. Stories often rise from the clash of moral voice and some sense of autonomy largely because they are a meaningful part of our creative struggle, individually and collectively, to bring about a new future. They have been around since time-before-remembering. The story and its people are one. Stories not only shape who we are, but also what we become; yet no boundaries hold the story. Just as each person is a collection of stories, so, too, is each community. Like the blooming globemallow and the striking prairie sunflower, stories give us pause to *be*. They help us pass down traditions. They teach us how to live off the land. They bring to life our customs and help us maintain our language, giving tribute to our beginnings so future generations may continue the legacy of our people. Stories define humanity, revealing deeper meaning within the rhythms and melodies of life that help us retrace the many-colored threads of our cultural past, a past woven in a tapestry that gives new meaning to its vivid expression in the present. Stories give the children their voice, and their eyes to *see*. Stories are words incarnate; they embody our imagination and give us something with flesh-and-blood ties to carry the rest of our days. Stories are good medicine, and communities need them for their healing power."

"Sani, it sounds like people who have walked before us left behind old trails to follow. Their stories provide lessons for the present that connect the-time-that-was-before to our future, and provide a glimpse into a way of life that has endured for generations. At first, it is as though there is no future; only a past. Without warning, we find ourselves back to the present where there seems to be nothing but time. Yet, it's in between where each story comes to life in ways that join us to the whole, where our *be*-ing overcomes our *do*-ing and our belonging is strengthened in each new beginning. If that's true, we soon become more like you, Sani."

"Like me, Topangah? How so?"

"That's easy. We become, at once, both the story and the teller. We are what our people need to hear. They see what we speak. They journey as much as a lifetime to arrive by our side, and they soon touch what isn't there as the storyteller literally becomes the story. Each ending marks another's beginning. And so the story unfolds, one day, one life, one breath, one weathered page at a time. It is for us only to listen to hear the voices echo loud, long, and far. And we haven't far to go to discover the voices return, bouncing off the canyon walls because they, like time, rise and fall in a circle where the future is part of our past, the past a foundation for our future."

"Well said, Topangah. Let me add, there are many journeys in one."

"How is that, Sani?"

"I have often heard it said among our people, 'It takes a thousand voices to tell a single story.' The power of stories is found in the feelings they summon among those gathered to hear them. Stories teach us about life, its purpose, and our path through it. With the tightness of a Navajo rug, they weave one great truth: we are to love one another. Topangah, *we* are the stories. We come from everywhere at once; everything is a part of us just as we are part of everything. That's why we are never alone, anywhere."

"I am glad we are never alone, Sani. I can not bear to think how sad I would be if I had to herd the sheep, clean the wool, or go to the corn fields alone during planting time in Spring's season of new life. And can you imagine what life would be like if I had no one to laugh and play with as I fetch water in a clay pot during Summer's growing season? The thought alone breaks my heart. And everyone knows it is good to have someone to talk to while sewing with an awl and sinew, or embroidering with quills of gull and porcupine dyed in colors that remind me of Autumn's season of ripening and harvest. And how could anyone want to be alone among the unflattering smells of sheep, wool, and wood smoke while dressing skins or cutting and making moccasins as cold winds cover our mother, the Earth, during the season of suffering, sorrow, and death we call Winter? Yet, we must remember, spring comes again to the sacred red earth. Oh, how sad it must be to travel the seasons alone."

"Especially when we don't have to, Topangah. If we but follow our intuition, circular and moving, we learn stories contain fragments of wisdom with the power to keep our hearts pure. Beaver would say to us, 'It is the present moment where wisdom is put to the most demanding test.' It's true wisdom can be funny, enlightening, and profound, yet it remains the same generation after generation, calling forth all we have learned and all we have accomplished so we might be better prepared to more adequately meet the challenges that come our way. Because wisdom cannot be bestowed, it must be cherished. As stories come to you, Topangah, care for them. They will help you bring wisdom out of the hearts of the people, and keep alive our ways. It is the fundamental nature of wisdom to *know* it is our stories, not wise words, that speak from one heart to another and draw us closer. To see the path ahead as a hand trembler (spiritual healer), teacher, and singer (medicine woman), your love — and your leadership — must walk with Wolf in humility. Humility is the one strength that unceasingly gives meaning to all the others. Its outward focus reminds us we are like our Great Elder Brother, *Chiye-Tanka* (Sabe), one who is honest to the natural laws of creation and to each other, embraces an uncommon humility, and is keenly aware we are but a small part of a larger world where, in the midst of chaos and confusion, we are neither inferior nor superior to another; we neither dominate nor are we dominated. As both Wolf and *Chiye-Tanka* demonstrate in their lives, humility recognizes that which belongs to one belongs to all; one holds no advantage over another. It is with great patience we learn to walk humbly, live simply, and serve ably the needs of another. Our place as a word sender (storyteller) is to listen closely to the vibrant voices rising like curling wisps of smoke beyond the old men and the old women who have walked before us, to help our people find themselves in life's single, sacred connection, and to honor our many Elders — Great Spirit; rocks, pebbles, and stones; plants and tall standing brothers;

animals, fish, and birds; Mother Earth, wind, fire, and water; Grandfather Sun; and humanity. Our stories, Topangah, occupy many dimensions. They bring the-past-beyond-the-past to a place within our reach so we may bring to life their lessons and rich meaning in a future waiting for our children and our children's children. Like our woven blankets, carved dolls, and celebration masks, stories fill the places and spaces of our lives with a power to reflect, teach, and heal. From the earthbound to the celestial, stories show us the way — the Beauty Way — and they guard our paths. Stories help us help one another."

"As you have helped me. Thank you, Sani, for all you have taught me these last several days."

"Topangah, we do not say 'thank you.' We say 'I am very happy from my heart for what you have done.' Besides, there is no need for that. We learn together."

"I am very happy from my heart for what you have done, Sani."

"And I am very happy to walk with you, Topangah. As we've discovered, sacredness, a hidden harmony, oft time comes to people in strange spaces. It is not something we can understand or explain. Instead, we become still and alert; only then can we truly be aware of the sacredness, the hidden harmony that is one with us, within and without. As we observe all that goes on around us, we come to see, hear, feel, and know *Hózhóó* — our ever-present religion. We call it *Beauty*, and it is as natural as breathing, eating, or walking. We are not separate from it. As we let go of conscious thought, we begin to sense and experience the hidden harmony that unfolds when we extend respect to all of nature and its many life forms and realign with the wholeness of life. An inability to see beauty, Topangah, doesn't mean it's not there. Buffalo teaches us the blade of grass shares the same desire to live, to grow, and to freely give — the same beauty — we possess. Beauty is like that; it's the natural state of the world and it demands balance. None is better than another. Everything is spiritual, yet nothing is spiritual. Beyond the walls humanity builds to segregate us by outward appearances, and beyond the borders we scratch into the earth to impose our varied cultures, norms, mores, languages, religions, beliefs, and collective will, we soon discover there are far many more things that bring us together than things that separate us. Though we are different in many small ways, we tend to share the same grand desires, dreams, and determination. At our essence, Topangah, we are similar; indeed, we are very much the same. We are brother and sister. We are one. As our awareness of this innate oneness grows, we grow more familiar with our surroundings; we begin to hear the language of the stones, and to feel vibrant color — the color-of-the-forest-in-spring, the color-of-the-sky, bright-as-a-flower color, the color-of-the-setting-sun — reverberate with the magnificent forces of nature. Only when we hear and feel do we begin to *see*. With our seeing comes learning. In our learning, we begin to understand it is for the singer — the spiritual healer, the teacher, the leader — to reflect, reaffirm, and respect the beauty of all life. There can be no balance, no beauty, no respect unless — and until — we learn how to listen to each other, to hear the truth. Let us, therefore, continue our walk in beauty."

"Where do we find truth, Sani? Can we find it in books? Does it belong only to special teachers, healers, leaders, or singers? Does it reside within the contours of one religion or another?"

"Topangah, it's simpler than that. The old Turtle would say, 'Truth endures, and it is never far away.' When the *Diné* come across truth, they feel it within their hearts. The same is true for all people. Truth comes from within; it is inside each of us. Every old man and every old woman, every young man, every young woman, and every child has truth. To see truth, we need only to look behind one's eyes. That's also where we see the other half of self. Balance awaits us there."

Topangah knows this place beneath the shadows of junipers and piñon trees as she knows herself. With the first important steps of her journey behind her, it is now for her to remember, and to follow Sani's footsteps of *know*-ing. As for the *Diné*, their watchful waiting is over. All who know Topangah have gathered to hear her story, a pure and eloquent story of great discovery brought to life in the midst of so many who love her and stand with her among the magnificent mesas of *Dinétah*.

"*Waneeshee*, Topangah." (May the way be forever beautiful for you.)

Those who looked for her arrival could not help but see the wonder of where she was. Something was different. Having already had her *kinaalda*, a Navajo girl's pure, powerful, and sacred rite of passage, Sani recently performed the *Hózhóójí*, or Blessing Way, to help ensure Topangah, now a Navajo woman, was fully capable of drawing connections to and from every aspect of Navajo life for her people, from spiritual and intellectual to social and physical. After all, Topangah was first a woman and, in that role, it is for her to maintain a Beauty Way of life, to pass down her culture, to set a good example, and to balance words and deeds. It is the only way to achieve Navajo harmony between traditional and contemporary life.

Now back among her people after four days on the mesa among the red buttes and rock spires that sit on the desert floor and reach toward blue skies, Sani announced, *"Díí beebi'dool zíí."* The people immediately knew it to mean, 'This one has a gift.'

Topangah's quest drew her closer to the people than she had ever been. She knew herself to be exceedingly loved, but she also knew something was somehow very different now. She was theirs, and nothing would ever be the same again.

After giving the *Diné* a few moments to express their delight and approval, Sani continued, telling those gathered around (everyone was gathered around!), *"Díí bidine'éyíká adoolwol"* (This one will help her people). "She will be a singer, a medicine woman."

Of course, the *Diné* knew Topangah as more than simply an emerging leader, and more than a spiritual healer, teacher, or a singer. Although she would never say as much, she is now a keeper of the wisdom, traditional faith, and philosophy of *iiná* — life — for the *Diné*. She is a storyholder. The *Diné* will look to her to retell the stories. Like few others, she is obligated to learn, hold, tell, and share the people's stories. She can choose to do so through the singing of songs, or the telling of tales. She can dance, or chant. The result is the same: her people are empowered and transformed. The *Diné* know stories change us if we are willing (and courageous enough) to put our fear of change (largely our selfish nature) aside. Stories, after all, connect us to those who walked this land before, leaving old trails for us to follow; like markers on life's pathway, stories confirm our journey, and our place upon it. Stories bring about a greater humility to help us instill a greater awareness, a greater knowledge, and a greater sensitivity to others. Stories and those who tell them are the great connectors of life.

Sani is a great connector of life. He knows of the old ways: buffalo and bear hunts, beaver traps, broken words and settlement papers that would take away our beloved *Dinétah*. As her thoughts swirled, Topangah spoke of her desires: "If I am to be part of a greater whole, I cannot ignore my relationships with beings outside my small understanding. Mine is a boundless nature. I have nothing; I am nothing. Yet, together, we share an abundance of everything. If I am to serve the *Diné*, it is for me to be here."

After many moons of intensive learning, Sani had no more to teach her. His job as a teacher would soon give way to his more important role as a mentor and grandfather. Topangah's teaching role, however, was just beginning. Speaking for all to hear, Sani's very words seem to burn and smoke as a tear on his cheek catches a glint of light: "Topangah, it is for you to put forward your steadfast dedication to the people, and to the land that is your home. It's time for you to walk the path of heart. Go now," Sani told her. "You have much to do."

With tears welling up in her own eyes, Topangah offers a soft 'Good-bye' to Sani. Before letting go of her hand, Sani gently whispers, "It is not for us to say 'good-bye' dear

Topangah. Instead, we say 'I'm going now, and I'll see you again.'"

With their parting, two become one in purpose, one in mind, one in spirit; one ageless with enduring knowledge, and one fledgling, only beginning yet filled with a marvelous, renewed hope. As Topangah turned to face the *Diné*, she smiled as a quiet love filled her soul.

After what seemed a very long time, she recalled something Sani told her as they left the village that first morning: "When leaders lead with love, the land is fresh, and the children smile."

"O' Great Spirit, grant us wisdom and teach us how we may honor and heal the earth and each other. Help us to know the human family has strayed away from the sacred way."

"O' Great Spirit, look past our brokenness. Give us eyes to see how the trees reach out and touch one another as they grow. Only then will we learn to reach out to someone, to touch them that we, too, may grow. Help us understand the Pine does not war with the Oak and there is sun enough for both. There is strength in our remembering. Help us remember one tree is not like another because it is their diversity that cultivates and nourishes their strength."

"O' Great Spirit, thank you for gentle winds and for hearts that listen to the worship of the trees among the bird's song. We are grateful to be part of creation. We know Mother Earth supports and cares for us through this life, and all men breathe the same air as the mountains. Help us stop to take notice of the world around us, to understand life is a gift and it is up to us to do something with it. We know our place among the winds and we know it is there we shall find our true colors, even if we have to walk against the winds to reach our destination."

"O' Great Spirit, we know we are divided, and we know it is mankind who must come back together to walk in the sacred way. There is a path our hearts must follow. It requires sacrifice. Lead us. Help us find the courage to willingly give ourselves to struggle so we may see more clearly the gift that comes from you, the gift of peace that comes to those who see the sacred colors of man blended into a single hue of humanity that shines like a hundred suns. Help us to feel the warmth from the light of so many suns, that we may rediscover love, compassion, and community."

"O' Great Spirit, as I lead the people, help me understand greatness is something that passes through me, not from me. Help me to lead with love."

Epilogue

I have been to the end of the Earth. I have been to the end of the waters.
I have been to the end of the sky. I have been to the end of the
mountains.
I have found none that are not my friends.
~Navajo chant

"Fairlight, I have so enjoyed these last couple of hours. I could just sit and listen to your stories for days on end. Do you mind me asking where I might find these stories in print? I'd love to share them with my family and friends."

"Ours is largely an oral tradition. Stories are passed from generation to generation. These particular stories were told to me by my mother's mother who, in turn, heard them first hand from her mother, Amá."

"Amá? The same Amá you bring to life in the stories you just shared?"

"Yes, that's right. Topangah is my great grandmother."

"How privileged we are to hear them now from you."

"Now that you've heard them, would you mind sharing what you found particularly striking?"

"Are you kidding, Fairlight? Lessons of life, love, and leadership infuse your stories with timeless truths. More than anything, your stories remind me of something Sophocles wrote many years ago: 'One word frees us of all the weight and pain of life: that word is love.' Of course, there is much we can learn about life, love, and leadership from wise men and women of every age. Growing up, I recall hearing stories of Tecumthe, more commonly referred to as Chief Tecumseh (Crouching Tiger) of the Shawnee Nation. I suppose that's because his teachings, very much in line with Sophocles' thinking, urge us to 'love our life, perfect our life, and beautify all things in our life.' Can you image what our world would look like if we heeded the message of these two great men and devoted our days to 'beautifying all things in our life?' I know, I know. In today's busy-ness, it's probably asking too much for us to slow down for such a romantic notion, but I think Sophocles was on to something. What better way to 'beautify life' than to color it with love?"

"Are you suggesting life is all about you and me and love, these three?"

"How incredibly insightful, Fairlight. I don't know that I've ever taken the time to think about life in those terms before. Nor do I think I've ever enjoyed lunch this much before. That sandwich was incredibly delicious, and this sweet, honey-oat pastry is divine. I must bring more of my friends here."

"You can bring me back anytime you'd like, too! This little coffee shop is quite lovely. Can I ask a question to help get us back on track?"

"Sure. Please do!"

"Have you ever thought about what is it, exactly, leaders *should* be doin'?"

"No. I can't say that I have, at least not consciously. Of course, I often wonder (I suppose I complain, too) about leaders who obviously are not doin', as you say, enough. I guess if I had to narrow down my desires, I'd want them to do more to remove the fear from my life and from our world."

"If I hear you right, you want leaders to be more about the people they serve, and you want them to be more about those things that scare us. Left untouched and not confronted, those scary things stand in the way of respect, trust, integrity, friendships, faith in one another, and hope. They stand in the way of life. And they stand in the way of you and me and love. To our dismay, fear, given its tendency to deceive, is quick to disguise itself behind long, thick curtains pretending to be something it is not."

"Please don't tell anyone, Fairlight, but those scary things sound a lot like a few 'leaders' I know."

"These 'curtains' (you know, scary things like where we come from, gender, socio-economic and class status, how we look, the color of our skin, life-style choices, religious leanings, political persuasions, and the like) often hang precariously from rusty nails in the cracked walls of man's inhumanity to man. Over time, they are jostled loose by the unrelenting march of time and the resolute persistence of the human will's desire to overcome. If we look carefully, the light of other-centered leadership majestically rises over the horizon, piercing these curtains to give us, with renewed clarity, a brief glimpse of the beauty that lies on the other side — a beauty that helps us 'see' what really matters — if we could only face our fear with good courage."

"So, what does really matter, Fairlight?"

"For me, what matters is who we are as people, what we do to help another, and what we need from those we have chosen to lead us."

"Are you saying we must make a conscious choice to follow?"

"Actually, I am saying something far more profound. It is for us to mindfully choose who shall lead us, a choice that will vary depending on our collective need and our circumstance. But there is more. When those we have chosen to lead us no longer lead, we must decide for ourselves whether we will turn from them and ask another to guide our steps. Choosing to follow and choosing how to be lead are two different things."

"Why is that, Fairlight?"

"There exists a prevailing sense that leadership has somehow lost its authenticity. In many corner offices, we find 'leaders' surrounded by what some refer to as 'good people with great talent and awesome attitudes.' It reminds me of Frank Baum's mysterious wizard of Oz in the Emerald City, where an ordinary man stands behind a curtain expending great effort to deceive, even if it is well-intended. Like the 'Wizard,' too many 'leaders' put on a show, of sorts, instilling fear in their quest to make themselves look good to investors and boards of directors, of all people, who, themselves' likely have only their own best interests at heart."

"Sorry to interrupt, Fairlight, but 'great talent and awesome attitudes' sound pretty good to me. What's wrong with it?"

"In simple terms, attitude reflects leadership. Left to their own devices, leaders more interested in highlighting 'outstanding' results, results that have little to do with talent or leadership, run the real risk of coming across as shallow, greedy, prejudiced, self-centered, and often badly presented. You see, if our job as leader is merely to gather 'good people with great talent and awesome attitudes' to benefit the few — the 'winning team,' if you will — what's left to do? Therein, of course, is our problem. We need only look to C-suites and senior executives around the globe (you know, teams of CEOs, COOs, CFOs, SVPs and the like) to see the calamity that befalls such thinking."

"Calamity? Is it really that bad, Fairlight?"

"Here's the lesson for me: those who would lead are confronted with the problem of authenticity. Top-down strategies that insist on surrounding the leader with 'good' people, fail to place the people first. By design, the leader becomes the center of attention. I'm reminded of a bygone era during the long, hot summer days on dusty, American grade school playgrounds when the two very best players stood in front of the rest of us selecting, one at a time, what he (yes, in those days, it was *always* a he) considered the best players available for his team. Sounds nice enough, I suppose, if your only interest is looking good and/or winning fame and admiration because you are so adept at gathering 'good people with great talent and awesome attitudes.' Of course, it doesn't look so good to the one left standing after everyone else has been selected. And it doesn't take into account the rest of us who are making judgments of our own as we look on from the sidelines."

"I remember those days, Fairlight."

"For me, the way to get attitudes to go up, up, up is not for leaders to select great talent predisposed with awesome attitudes but, rather, to take on the challenge of first improving their own attitude. 'Attitude,' Winston Churchill taught years ago, 'is a little thing that makes a big difference.' You see, with the right leadership — an other-centered leadership — people of *all* walks of life can come to terms with their differences, leverage their strengths to build synergies that overcome a long history of fear, hostility, and mistrust, sacrifice self for others (indeed, for a better humanity), dream their very own dreams, and come together to achieve great things, even if they are not very good at the game. That's what leadership does. And that's what life is about."

"I don't know if I ever thought about it that way, Fairlight."

"Give the notion a test spin. Next time teams are being forged on the school playground in your community, look for those leaders who go out of their way to pick players not based on any great talent but, instead, on their love of the game and their desire to be part of the team, whether they can play or not. That will be the team that learns the most, loves the most, and has the most fun because that's the team that stands on the shoulders of a true leader. That is the team that comes to a better understanding of what life holds in store for all of us. They may not win on the scoreboard, but they'll be chalking up some heavy points in the game of life. And it will not take others long to notice."

"Now that's leadership!"

"It's more than that, really. Love brings this kind of leadership to life. The good news is leadership like this comes in all colors, shapes, and sizes because love comes in all colors, shapes, and sizes. To borrow the words of Aeschylus, an ancient Greek poet and playwright born 2,500 years ago, such a leader is sure to 'tame the savageness of man and make gentle the life of this world.' Maybe I'm a bit naïve, but it seems to me *that's* the job leaders ought to be doin'."

"I think so, too, but can I ask something? If that's the job leaders *ought* to be doin', why aren't they doin' it? Are we witnessing a failure of leadership, Fairlight?"

"I don't think it's a failure of leadership but, rather, a failure on the part of those who seek to lead to understand what, exactly, the rest of us are looking for."

"What does that mean, Fairlight?"

"In short, it means the leader must fully understand the people in order to be one with them. With that understanding, we are awakened and cannot help but to love. Yet, we have it in our heads leaders are supposed to come into our lives and unpack some 'compelling' vision of the future the rest of us, they think, want to see. Trouble is, that's not leading; that's selling. Besides, a vision is not a leader's to give, only uncover. The people already have a vision. The only way a leader can discover and articulate the vision closely held in the people's hearts is to take the time and make the effort to get to know who the people really are, and where it is the people want to go. Only when the leader understands the people's hearts will they come to understand it is not a leader the people seek; instead, they seek to know love."

"I wish more leaders fully understood this, Fairlight."

"I have heard it said the future comes to us from the past, but not in a straight line. And it scares us. It also scares the leaders among us. Predictability, as it were, is seen as some kind of cure for our fears. But, if I may ask, what is there to fear? After all, we can see both directions from the bend of the road. With this awareness, we come to know what is going on, not only here but also there, and we awaken to the change prompted by our life's work, that of finding truth. Within this truth we find *our* way that others may follow. Carl von Clausewitz, a Prussian soldier, military theorist, and classical strategic thinker at the turn of the nineteenth century, describes this moment as *coup d'oeil*: 'the rapid discovery of a truth which to the ordinary mind is either not visible at all or only becomes so after long examination and reflection.' Those who possess a modicum of belief that, in the end, truth must prevail, find solace in their journey, somehow knowing the well-worn path that promotes the public good also finds a way, however fragile, to ignite a spark of life to promulgate truth. So, what is this 'truth' we so intently seek? To what extent do we share the same truth? What might this truth have to do with the meaning of life? One view, suggests Kahlil Gibran, a Lebanese-American artist, poet, and writer of the early twentieth century, teaches 'God made truth with many doors to welcome every believer who knocks on them.' That said, our problem becomes one of discovery. 'Truth, when not sought after,' Oliver Wendell Holmes emphasizes, 'rarely comes to light.' No matter how many doors, we must first seek and, in finding, knock. How else will we know what we have found?"

"I think I'll be spending a lot more time appreciating where the road bends, Fairlight. How will we know we have found our truth?"

"In our quest to find truth, listen for the music."

"Music?"

"Yes. Music, it has been said, 'is what life sounds like.' Ronald Reagan, the 40th President of the United States, called life 'one grand, sweet song.' Do you know Louis Armstrong, a renowned jazz trumpeter and singer from New Orleans? He reminds us, 'What we play is life.' To find our music — and our life — we must first suspend our longing for it. In our stillness, fear subsides, and. humanity breaks into a big, wide-eyed, childlike smile because her melodious opus is more complete, eager to resound in all of her glory!"

"Music is a lovely metaphor for life, Fairlight. Having found life, what more is there?"

"Well, that's just it, my friend. The Apache says, 'You must speak straight so that your words may go as sunlight into our hearts.' Our search for truth brings us face to face with life's symphony. And we see with our hearts the beautiful music. Everything we see is beautiful. Buddha would calmly but wisely propose the truth we seek is, undeniably, beauty. 'Love is beauty and beauty is truth,' he teaches us, 'and that is why in the beauty of a flower we can see the truth of the universe.' Did you catch it?"

"Catch what, Fairlight?"

"If love is beauty and beauty is truth, doesn't it stand to reason love is the truth we seek? 'Love,' Alexander Smith, a Scottish poet of the mid-nineteenth century, would say, 'is but the discovery of ourselves in others, and the delight in the recognition.' According to Henry Ward Beecher, a prominent abolitionist, clergyman, and social reformer of Smith's era, 'Love is the river of life in the world.' With this insight, we find ourselves where we started, and where we first learned life is you and me and love, these three, with a little music, of course, thrown in for good measure."

"You are very well-read, Fairlight."

"I'd rather like to think there are few things that matter more than life and love, and you and me, and the role leaders play in matters of such importance."

"Fairlight, what do you think love is, exactly?"

"Many believe love is a feeling that overcomes them when they least expect it. Others look at it more as an obligation, a duty if you will. But love is so much more. The ancient Greeks devised four words to help capture the vastness of love. *Eros*, as we know, is the love that gets our fires burning. *Storge* is the love warmly shared by a parent and child, a familial love. *Philia* is a love most often associated with great friendship. Did you know Philadelphia,

Pennsylvania, is heralded as the city of 'brotherly love?' If we look closely, these first three terms for love reflect a deep, emotional attachment. Paul, a first-century Roman citizen and Hebrew Pharisee from the Mediterranean city of Tarsus, describes the fourth aspect, *agape*, in his letter to the cosmopolitan residents of Corinth some 2,000 years ago. In this letter, we learn,

> Love is patient, love is kind. It does not envy, it does not boast, it is not proud. It is not rude, it is not self-seeking, it is not easily angered, it keeps no record of wrongs. Love delights not in evil but rejoices with the truth. It always protects, always trusts, always hopes, always perseveres.

Agape is a love that not only loves, but also gives ... because it wants to. Agape gives expecting nothing in return. Agape is other-centered; it is about self-denial for the sake of another. Alan Redpath, a British author and evangelist, describes this love as 'the actual absorption of our being in one great passion.'"

"That sounds wonderful, Fairlight. Can you tell me more?"

"I am personally fond of what Martin Luther King, Jr., has to say about the matter. He reminds us, 'Love is the only force capable of transforming an enemy into a friend.'"

"Do you think love can do that, Fairlight?"

"I certainly do."

"But, how, Fairlight?"

"Quite simply, it covers, or bears, all things. When you think about love, you realize it never brings discredit for someone's wrong-doing. Charles Spurgeon, a nineteenth century British preacher, said, 'Love stands in the presence of a fault with a finger on her lip.' I just love that image, and I can't help but to think love nudges us in but one direction, to continually look for the good in others."

"Do you know why, Fairlight?"

"Of course, I do my beautiful friend. It's because we are certain to find it. But that's not all we'll find. You see, love always hopes for the best; it never gives up. It's warm, welcoming, and radiates a gentleness that invites others to partake of its sweetness."

"Has much changed in the way people see love today?"

"I don't think so. Have you heard of the Black-Eyed Peas, an American hip hop group from Los Angeles, California? Among other things, they sing of love. Their inspiring message of 'one race, one love, one people' exudes a gentle power that transcends the ages. In teaching we are an important part of the whole, its message resonates with people of all walks of life; every color and all shapes and sizes. Theirs is a message vibrantly wrapped with hope, and meticulously distilled to a call for action. It connects all of us, heart to heart. In bringing us face to face with something bigger than ourselves, it sets us free! It compels us to act in a way that rises above the warn out ritual of tit for tat. It cries out for us to do more to transform our world, to go beyond free hugs, giving a homeless man a couple of bucks, or offering casual allegiance to a religion. Ours is a mad, mad world, and our actions would do good to reflect that reality. Friedrich Wilhelm Nietzsche, a German philosopher, composer, and poet of the late nineteenth century, recognized 'there is always some madness in love. But there is also always some reason in madness.' We live in a constant state of change. Chaos births our madness, it seems, and gives reason to our love."

"There's madness in love? Are you serious?"

"Indeed. Few there are who, I believe, would disagree with the necessity for reason, even in madness. Consider nature. Someone suggested, 'If nothing ever changed, there'd be no butterflies.' Yet, we learn from Richard Buckminster Fuller, a twentieth century American author, architect, engineer, inventor, futurist, and systems theorist, 'There is nothing in a caterpillar that tells you it's going to be a butterfly.' Because we can see in the caterpillar a great, lonely struggle to set itself free and become a butterfly, the truth we share with Thomas Mann, a German novelist, social critic, and Nobel Prize laureate, is self-evident: 'it is love, not reason, that is stronger than death.' We, in many ways like the caterpillar, stand face to face with the struggles of a new day in full view of the freedom that awaits us if we act upon our courage, not because madness wreaks havoc in our world but, rather, because love subdues the madness. Love is not provoked into unkindness; it unites us as one. Martin Luther King, Jr. puts love into perspective, teaching us, 'Hatred paralyzes life, love releases it. Hatred confuses life, love harmonizes it. Hatred darkens life, love illumines it.'"

"All this talk of arduous struggle, hatred, and death makes me wonder how love ever survived. It did survive, didn't it, Fairlight?"

"You know the answer to that question. Of course, it survived. Madness was with us long before the dawn of time. So, too, was love. Love will be with us long after madness fades away; love never fails. In the end, those who love are bigger than the madness and can see it for what it is. Those who love can forgive its trespass, its stumbles and staggers, and its fall. 'Forgiveness,' as Reinhold Niebuhr, a prominent American theological ethicist, so eloquently puts it, 'is the final form of love.' Agape, you see, does not love in order to receive. Sure, one can express this love by giving all they possess so others may have food. One can even go so far as to give their life so others may have life, even abundantly. But such great personal sacrifice is not the measure we seek. Love is its own measure. And, as R&B singer Mary J. Blige so poignantly sings from her album, *Share My World*, 'love is all we need.'"

"Fairlight, that's beautiful. I am a huge fan of Mary J. Blige and Rhythm & Blues. Come to think of it, I have that album! But tell me, what's all this stuff about love got to do with leadership?"

"Across the vast sea of time, great leaders in all cultures emerge first as servants. There have been leaders for as long as people have built communities. But one kind of leader, a serving leader, stands apart. That's because the nature of serving leadership derives its power from the people and, by extension, the authority of a serving leader is the esteem of the people. Its traditions hail from the Middle East and the Orient."

"Really? I had no idea."

"Let's take a closer look. In ancient Hebrew texts written 3,500 years ago, Moses, a high ranking prince in the palace of Pharaoh and heir to the proudest throne on earth, renounced the richness of his life — and his inheritance —to serve Hebrew slaves and lead them out of Egyptian bondage. Some 500 years later, Rehoboam was a king of ancient Israel and later king of the Kingdom of Judah after the ten northern tribes of Israel rebelled to form the independent Kingdom of

Israel. Seeking advice from those who stood before Solomon, King Rehoboam was encouraged 'to be a servant unto his people, to serve them and answer them, and speak good words unto them.' Lao Tzu, in the 6th century BC, said, 'I have three precious things which I hold fast and prize. The first is gentleness; the second is frugality; the third is humility, which keeps me from putting myself before others. Be gentle and you can be bold; be frugal and you can be liberal; avoid putting yourself before others and you can become a leader among men.'"

"I must admit it's not easy for me to associate gentleness and humility with leadership these days. And to think a King would serve the people is far from what one would expect in twenty-first century Western society. Do we have other examples, Fairlight?"

"Sure. Chanakya, an Indian writer and political strategist some 2,400 years ago, writing in the *Arthashāstra*, explains the Indian way of life in terms vastly similar to today's general concept of servant leadership. For them, the walk mattered more than the talk. We learn, 'The king shall consider as good not what pleases himself but what pleases his subjects.' About 400 years later, Jesus, a Jewish teacher from Galilee during the Roman occupation of Judea, urged others to be servants first, reminding them, 'You know the rulers, how they lord over the people, and their high officials exercise authority over them. Not so with you. Whoever wants to become great among you must be a servant, and whoever wants to be first must be a slave.' True leadership, we learn from the Lakotah, is only possible when character is more important than authority. Not so many years ago, a Georgia preacher encouraged others to seek greatness through service and love. In a sermon delivered shortly before his murder, Martin Luther King, Jr., taught, 'If you want to be important — Wonderful! If you want to be recognized — Wonderful! If you want to be great — Wonderful! But recognize he who is greatest among you shall be your servant. ... you only need a heart full of grace and a soul generated by love to be that servant.'"

"This is fascinating, Fairlight. I had no idea we could learn so much about life and love through leadership. Is there more?"

"Sam Ervin, a United States Senator from North Carolina, said, 'A person who is worthy of being a leader wants power not for himself, but in order to be of service.'

The serving nature of leadership, I believe, is written on our hearts as a natural law. Stephen Covey, an American author, businessman, and educator, says 'the power to cultivate servant leadership comes from the individual. It's an inside-out approach.' For me, it originates from a servant's heart."

"What's a servant's heart, Fairlight? I don't think I've ever heard leadership put in that context before."

"Have you read Paul Hawken's book, *Blessed Unrest?* He writes, 'an older quiescent history is reemerging, what poet Gary Snyder calls *the great underground,* a current of humanity that dates back to the Paleolithic. Its lineage can be traced back to healers, priestesses, philosophers, monks, rabbis, poets, and artists who speak for the planet, for other species, for interdependence, a life that courses under and through and around empires.' What stands out for me among this reemerging history is the quiet nature of her leaders. Have you ever wondered why we think power, prestige, position, and privilege equate to leadership? Or why we think the owner, the boss, the CEO, the President, the Pope, the senior pastor, the chairman of the board, or the Secretary General is *the* leader? Is it because a quiet grace struggles to coexist? We want strength in our leaders, failing to see meekness and gentleness — the essence of a quiet grace — are among the most reliable indicators of strength. Of course, it's generally pretty easy to determine what happens when leadership rests upon power, prestige, position, or privilege. A more important question to ask is what, exactly, doesn't happen? After all, it's usually the leader's vision we are asked to adopt. In so many ways, it's also *their*, game, *their* toys, and probably *their* rules. The only thing left to captivate, inspire, motivate, and encourage us is *their* personality. So a great many of us — some enthusiastically, others reluctantly — merely saddle up for the ride, hoping against hope the scenery has something of interest to offer along the way. Comparing *their* reality with the hope of the unseen, Hawken points to a great 'coalescence comprising hundreds of thousands of organizations' giving 'support and meaning' to billions of people, largely unseen, around the globe, that includes 'families in India, students in Australia, farmers in France, the landless in Brazil, the Bananeras of Honduras, the *poors* of Durban, villagers in Irian Jaya, indigenous tribes of Bolivia, and housewives in Japan.' Ever wonder who is leading *them*? Hawken knows. Their leaders, he tells us, are 'farmers, zoologists, shoemakers, and poets.'"

"Farmers, zoologists, shoemakers, and poets? Are you kidding? That's incredible. No CEOs? Are you certain? No President or Chairman of the Board? Surely there must be some mistake. No members of Parliament either? What about the Congress? Or, maybe the Senate?"

"None of that. Ever wondered why self-proclaimed leaders might relinquish control of this vast underground? It's quite simple, actually. Dr B.R. Ambedkar, a 20th century philosopher, thinker, anthropologist, historian, crusader for social justice, champion of human rights, and chief architect of the Indian Constitution, tells us why:

> A great man is different from an eminent one in that he is ready to be the servant of the society."

"That pretty much sums it up, doesn't it, Fairlight?"

"Such is a servant's heart. Do you know leaders like Ambedkar describes, leaders who consistently — indeed, relentlessly — place others before self? Leaders who possess a servant's heart? Leaders who perfectly understand the vision was never theirs to give; instead, it always belongs to the people, it always represents our common bond? Thomas

Carlyle, a nineteenth century Scottish writer, historian, and teacher, argued 'the history of the world is but a biography of great men.' But I have to wonder if a focus on leaders somehow failed to consider 'greatness' originates in the hearts of those who choose to follow? Martin Luther King, Jr., reminds us, 'Everyone can be great, because everyone can serve.'"

"So, if everyone can serve, can everyone lead?"

"I believe so, if they are to take a mind to it. Besides, it seems to me we could use a few million more 'great' leaders! Our world is in desperate need of a new generation of great leaders — like Topangah — stepping out to transmogrify our collective vision, reviving a distant dream to create the present reality, a reality founded on love. Leaders who have the power to reach the hearts of others understand, in the end, love is what we need."

"That's so beautiful, Fairlight. I would follow a leader like that anywhere because they understand leadership is not positional, it's relative. They also make it relevant and real. Such is the leader who turns Western society's autocratic, hierarchical command and control on its head, recognizing popularity, power, prestige, position, politics, perks, and privilege never are important; people are!"

"So, what does it meant to say everyone can lead, Fairlight?"

"Let me suggest leadership is relationship, a journey those who choose to be led share with those they choose to lead them. It is up to the people to determine who, in their hearts, has the capability to lead them, who truly understands their needs and is awakened to a shared love. John C. Maxwell, a present-day author and pastor, teaches, 'The measure of a leader is not the number of people who serve the leader, but the number of people served by the leader.'"

"That's a remarkable way of looking at leadership, Fairlight. I guess it's important to remember leadership doesn't just happen."

"That's right. Marian Anderson is a goodwill ambassador, a delegate to the United Nations Humanitarian Rights committee, a recipient of the Presidential Medal of Freedom, and a celebrated African-American singer. She has learned first hand, 'Leadership should be born out of the understanding of the needs of those who would be affected by it.' American Indian wisdom can help us. Our Shawnee friends of the American Midwest teach, 'Seek to make your life long and its purpose in the service of your people,' while our Kiowa brothers and sisters of the Great Plains put it this way: 'A leader is a servant of the people.' The Lakotah take leadership and service to a whole new level, suggesting, 'Those who live for one another learn that love is the bond of perfect unity.'"

"So, why lead, Fairlight?"

"It seems to me the fulfillment of leadership is the gratification of knowing that all of your efforts paid off in helping other people. Martin Luther King, Jr., put it this way: 'I question and soul-search constantly into myself to be certain as I can that I am fulfilling the true meaning of my work, that I am maintaining my sense of purpose, that I am holding fast to my ideals, and that I am guiding my people in the right direction.' As I see it, some of the best leaders are those that lead by being led. Perhaps that's because a leader needs the people more than the people need a leader."

"That's an interesting thing to say, Fairlight, but I have to ask, why does a leader need the people more than the people need a leader?"

"It's because leadership — true leadership — is love manifest, and leadership without love is no leadership at all."

"Fairlight, I have so enjoyed my time with you today. Thank you so much for sharing your love and leadership with me. You have given me much to contemplate as I do my small part to restore the love in our organization. I've much to do, and I can't wait to get started!

Acknowledgements

I have seen that in any great undertaking it is not enough for a man to depend simply upon himself.
~Isna-la-wica (Lone Man), Teton (Sioux)

My name is on the cover, but this work required far more than the effort of a single man can accomplish. Without significant contributions from a number of friends and family, there would be no book. I am grateful to all who have crossed my path, walked by my side, and shared this deeply personal journey with me.

From the beginning, my biggest fan and greatest source of inspiration came from my fabulous daughter, Gretl. She helped bring Topangah to life!

A long list of friends, many of them arriving in my life through the power of social media, has kept me company on this journey. None more so than Dr Steve Broe, Stan Faryna, Chad Sansing, James (Jim) Strock, and Harry Tucker. Thank you for walking with me. I am also indebted to so many who gave freely of their time, energy, and love expecting nothing in return. Kindness after kindness greeted me with valuable contributions large and small. To each of the following, a veritable who's who of world-class leaders, I'd like to express my sincere appreciation and heartfelt thanks: Wayne Adkins (Chickahominy), Majeed Al-Barghouthi, John Anderson, Roy Atkinson, PMH Atwater, Teri Aulph, Marilou Awiakta (Cherokee), Rick Bayless, Rebel Brown, S Max Brown, Dr Richard Brownlee, Deb Bruser, Bob Burg, Louis Campbell (Lumbee), Dave Carpenter, Brigadier General (ret) Fred Castle, Marion Chapsal, Teresa Cherfane, Dr Norman Cigar, Alan Cohn, Dorothy Dalton, Angela 'Silver Star' Daniel (Mattaponi), Catherine Darnell, Monica Diaz, Tim Douglas, Sharon Eden, Dr Norm Evans, George Fitz-Hugh, Edie Galley, Dr Stuart Gothold, Earl Gray, Jane Gunn, Kristy Hall, Les Haughton, Mike Henry, Robert Hull, Mark Hundley, Gerardo Jimenez, Steve Keating, Nannette Kennedy, Randall Krause, Ben Lichtenwalner, Liz Lynch, Lashawn 'SugaRay' Marston, Kurt Matheson, Susan Mazza,

Mark McKinney, Michael McKinney, Kalil Mohammed, Kevin Monroe, Lisa Morison, Shawn Murphy, Brandon Nater, Felix Nater, Toan Nguyen, John Noble, Karen Noles, Mark Oakes, Kevin O'Connor, Douglas Olson, Mary Phillips, Jane Purdue, Pierre Redmon, Mandy Rivera, Sarah Robinson, Dr Marion Ross, Mary Ann Ruehling, Marjorie 'Sunflower' Sargent (Mattaponi), Susan Steinbrecher, Janice Tanton, Dr Gerardo Vakero, Rachel Vigour, Laura Woodworth, and Dr Terry Woodworth.

Above all, my heart is grateful for the love, support, patience, and kindness graciously showered upon me day after glorious day by the love of my life, my wife and best friend, Wendy.

To all, Waneeshee (may the Way be Beauty-full for you).

www.ingramcontent.com/pod-product-compliance
Lightning Source LLC
Chambersburg PA
CBHW071416170526
45165CB00001B/295